BATTLEFIELD TO BOARDROOM

Leadership insight

from the Mahabharata

Manoj Sam & Jay Kumar

ISBN: 978-1-7323740-6-5

Published by

INDUS NETWORK

Fort Myers, Florida 33913

प्रथमे नार्जिता विद्या द्वितीये नार्जितं धनम् ।
तृतीये नार्जितं पुण्यं चतुर्थे किं करिष्यसि ॥

What can you do in the fourth part of your life,

when you have not gained knowledge in the first,

virtue in the second, and merit in the third?

Subhashita Manjari – 14.265

Bhima's Unconventional Tactics

Introduction

The Mahabharata, one of the most revered and ancient texts in Indian literature, is not just a tale of kings and wars but a treasure trove of wisdom and insights into human nature, governance, and strategic thinking. At its core, the Mahabharata is a story of the great Kurukshetra war, fought between the Pandavas and the Kauravas, but its lessons extend far beyond the battlefield. This book delves deep into the strategic and tactical aspects of the Mahabharata, exploring the decisions, actions, and consequences of its characters through a strategic lens. By examining the strategic maneuvers, leadership styles, and decision-making processes of key figures such as Krishna, Arjuna, Yudhishthira, and others, this book seeks to distill timeless lessons that can be applied to modern-day strategic challenges in various fields.

(a). The Wisdom of the Ancients:

Extracting Management Lessons

The ancient texts and epics of human history, such as the Mahabharata, offer a treasure trove of wisdom that transcends time and culture. The strategic insights, ethical dilemmas, and leadership examples found within these stories are not only fascinating from a historical perspective but also highly relevant to contemporary management practices. By extracting management lessons from these ancient sources, modern leaders can gain a deeper understanding of timeless principles that can enhance their effectiveness and the success of their organizations.

Vision and Strategic Foresight

One of the most compelling aspects of the Mahabharata is its emphasis on vision and strategic foresight. Lord Krishna's ability to foresee the outcomes of various actions and guide the Pandavas accordingly is a lesson in the importance of having a clear vision and long-term strategic planning. In modern management, leaders must be able to anticipate future trends, understand the broader context of their industry, and develop a strategic vision that aligns with the long-term goals of their organization. This involves not only setting a direction but also inspiring and mobilizing the team to work towards that shared vision.

Ethical Leadership and Integrity

The Mahabharata places a strong emphasis on ethics and morality, particularly through characters like Yudhishthira, who embodies integrity and adherence to dharma (righteousness). In today's business environment, ethical leadership is crucial. Leaders must navigate complex moral landscapes and make decisions that uphold the values and principles of their organization. By prioritizing ethics and integrity, leaders build trust with stakeholders, foster a positive organizational culture, and ensure sustainable long-term success.

Adaptability and Resilience

The journey of the Pandavas, filled with trials and tribulations, underscores the importance of adaptability and resilience. Modern managers can draw parallels to the need for flexibility in responding to changing market conditions, economic uncertainties, and unforeseen challenges. Resilience in management means maintaining a positive outlook, learning from setbacks, and continuously adapting strategies to meet evolving demands. This resilience is vital for sustaining growth and overcoming adversity in the business world.

Strategic Use of Information

Krishna's use of intelligence and information during the Kurukshetra war illustrates the power of data-driven decision-making. In the contemporary business context, the ability to gather, analyze, and utilize information effectively is a critical skill. Leaders must be adept at leveraging market research, customer insights, and competitive intelligence to inform their strategies and decisions. This strategic use of information enables organizations to stay ahead of the curve, capitalize on opportunities, and mitigate risks.

Team Building and Collaboration

The unity and collaboration among the Pandavas highlight the importance of strong team dynamics. Effective management involves building cohesive teams that work well together, leveraging each member's strengths, and fostering a collaborative environment. Modern leaders can learn from the Pandavas' example by promoting teamwork, encouraging open communication, and aligning individual efforts with collective goals. This creates a synergistic effect, where the whole is greater than the sum of its parts.

Crisis Management

The Mahabharata provides numerous examples of crisis management, particularly through Yudhishthira's composure and Krishna's strategic interventions. Modern leaders can benefit from understanding how to manage crises effectively by staying calm, making swift and informed decisions, and maintaining clear and empathetic communication. Effective crisis management involves anticipating potential challenges, preparing contingency plans, and leading with confidence and resilience during turbulent times.

Ethical Resource Allocation

The concept of dharma in the Mahabharata also extends to the ethical allocation and management of resources. Leaders are tasked with making decisions that balance short-term gains with long-term sustainability and ethical considerations. By applying principles of fairness, transparency, and responsibility, managers can ensure that resources are utilized efficiently and in a manner that benefits all stakeholders.

(b). Overview of the Book's Structure and Purpose

The book is structured into several chapters, each focusing on a different aspect of strategic thinking as portrayed in the Mahabharata. The chapters are designed to be both informative and engaging, drawing parallels between the epic narrative and contemporary strategic issues.

The first section of the book examines the visionary leadership of King Dhritarashtra, the blind king of Hastinapura, and how his inability to see the consequences of his actions led to the downfall of his dynasty. It also looks at the setting of objectives, drawing lessons from Arjuna's quest for knowledge and self-realization before the war.

The second section delves into the strategies crafted by Krishna, the divine charioteer and advisor to the Pandavas, and how his counsel influenced the outcome of the war. It also examines the competitive strategy on the battlefield, analyzing the strengths and weaknesses of both the Kaurava and Pandava forces.

The third section focuses on the tactical flexibility displayed by various characters in the epic, such as Arjuna's mastery of different weapons and Bhima's quick thinking in challenging situations. It also looks at how the Pandavas adapted to changing circumstances and seized opportunities to gain an advantage over their adversaries.

Overall, the book aims to provide readers with a deeper understanding of strategic thinking through the lens of one of the world's greatest epics, offering insights that are relevant and applicable in today's complex and dynamic world.

1.

Strategic Planning in the Mahabharata

In the epic Mahabharata, strategic planning plays a central role in shaping the outcomes of battles, alliances, and the fate of kingdoms. The epic is replete with examples of visionary leadership, clear objective setting, and strategic thinking, all of which are exemplified by key characters such as King Dhritarashtra, Arjuna, and Lord Krishna. This essay explores the strategic planning principles and lessons derived from their actions and decisions, highlighting the timeless wisdom that can be applied to contemporary leadership and management practices.

1.(A)

Visionary Leadership

Insights from King Dhritarashtra

Once upon a time, in the ancient land of Hastinapur, there ruled a king named Dhritarashtra. Blind since birth, his physical sightlessness was often said to mirror the darkness that lingered within his heart.

Despite his blindness, King Dhritarashtra possessed a keen intellect and a profound understanding of the world around him. However, his wisdom was clouded by his insatiable attachment to power and his eldest son, Duryodhana.

As the years passed, Dhritarashtra's kingdom teetered on the brink of chaos. Duryodhana, consumed by ambition and jealousy, sought to claim the throne for himself at any cost. Yet, blinded by his love for his son, Dhritarashtra turned a blind eye to Duryodhana's atrocities.

One fateful day, a sage named Vyasa visited the palace. With divine insight, Vyasa peered into the depths of Dhritarashtra's soul and saw the truth that lay buried beneath layers of desire and attachment.

"You are the king of a great kingdom, Dhritarashtra," Vyasa said, his voice carrying the weight of ages. "But your blindness is not in your eyes, it is in your heart. Your attachment to power and your son has clouded your judgment, leading you astray."

Dhritarashtra listened, his heart heavy with the weight of Vyasa's words. For the first time, he realized the folly of his ways. He had allowed his attachment to blind him to the suffering of his people, to the injustice perpetrated by his own son.

With newfound clarity, Dhritarashtra vowed to rectify his mistakes. He called upon his advisors and sought their counsel, determined to restore order and justice to his kingdom.

But the path ahead was fraught with challenges. Duryodhana, drunk with power, refused to yield, plunging the kingdom into a devastating war. As the battle raged on, Dhritarashtra watched helplessly, torn between his duty as a king and his love for his son.

In the end, the war exacted a heavy toll on both sides. Hastinapur lay in ruins, its once-proud halls reduced to rubble. Amidst the carnage, Dhritarashtra stood amidst the ashes of his kingdom, his heart heavy with grief and regret.

Yet, amidst the devastation, there flickered a glimmer of hope. For in his darkest hour, Dhritarashtra had gained a profound insight into the nature of power and attachment. He realized that true wisdom lay not in the pursuit of power, but in the service of others.

And so, with the dawn of a new day, Dhritarashtra embarked on a journey of redemption. He dedicated the remainder of his days to rebuilding his kingdom and serving his people with humility and compassion, his blindness now a symbol of the inner light that guided his path.

King Dhritarashtra's story would be remembered not for the mistakes of his past, but for the wisdom he gained from them. For in the end, it was his journey from darkness to light that truly defined his legacy.

☞ Key Lessons

1. **The Importance of Vision and Foresight:** Dhritarashtra's physical blindness is a powerful metaphor for his lack of foresight. Despite being surrounded by wise counselors like Vidura and Sanjaya, he failed to envision the long-term consequences of his actions and the actions of his son, Duryodhana. His inability to see beyond the immediate resulted in decisions that ultimately led to the great war of Kurukshetra.

2. **The Dangers of Favoritism:** Dhritarashtra's favoritism towards his son Duryodhana blinded him to his son's flaws and ambitions. This bias skewed his judgment and prevented him from taking necessary corrective actions. Dhritarashtra's indulgence allowed Duryodhana's malice to fester, leading to the estrangement and eventual war with the Pandavas.

3. **The Cost of Indecision:** Dhritarashtra is often portrayed as a leader who struggled with indecision. His desire to maintain peace within his family, even at the cost of justice and fairness, rendered him incapable of making firm decisions. This indecisiveness contributed to the outbreak of the Kurukshetra war, as he failed to address the escalating conflict between the Kauravas and Pandavas.

4. **Listening to Wise Counsel:** Despite having access to some of the wisest individuals in the epic, such as Vidura and Krishna, Dhritarashtra often chose to ignore their advice. His attachment to his son and his own insecurities led him to make poor decisions. For modern leaders, it is essential to recognize the value of wise counsel and to surround themselves with advisors who can provide honest and strategic advice.

1.(B)

Setting Objectives

Learning from Arjuna's Quest

In the ancient land of Kurukshetra, where legends were born and destinies intertwined, there lived a warrior named Arjuna. Renowned for his skill with the bow and arrow, Arjuna was a prince of the noble Kuru dynasty, destined for greatness.

Yet, despite his prowess on the battlefield, Arjuna found himself beset by doubt and confusion. As he stood on the eve of the great Kurukshetra War, gazing across the vast expanse of the battlefield, his heart grew heavy with uncertainty.

"What is the purpose of this war?" Arjuna wondered, his mind clouded by fear and hesitation. "How can I raise my weapon against my own kin and kin?"

In his moment of doubt, Arjuna turned to his charioteer, Lord Krishna, for guidance. With infinite patience and wisdom, Krishna imparted unto Arjuna the teachings of dharma and duty, revealing the true nature of the universe and the path to enlightenment.

"Seek not victory or defeat, Arjuna," Krishna counseled. "But strive instead for righteousness and justice. Fulfill your duty as a warrior, but do not be attached to the fruits of your actions."

Inspired by Krishna's words, Arjuna embarked on a journey of self-discovery and enlightenment. He learned to let go of his fears and attachments, embracing his duty as a warrior with courage and conviction.

As the war raged on, Arjuna fought with valor and integrity, his bow singing with the fury of a thousand winds. Yet, amidst the chaos and carnage of battle, he remained steadfast in his commitment to righteousness, never wavering from the path of dharma.

In the end, the forces of righteousness emerged victorious, and Arjuna stood triumphant upon the battlefield, his heart at peace and his soul ablaze with the fire of enlightenment.

Arjuna's quest would be remembered not for the battles he won or the enemies he vanquished, but for the lessons he learned along the way. For in the crucible of war, amidst the clash of steel and the cries of the fallen, Arjuna discovered the true meaning of life and the eternal truth that lies at the heart of all creation.

As the sun set on the battlefield of Kurukshetra, Arjuna looked upon the world with eyes unclouded by fear or doubt. For he had learned that true victory lies not in the conquest of others, but in the conquest of self. And in that moment of perfect clarity, Arjuna knew that he had finally found the path to enlightenment.

☞Key Lessons

1. **Embrace Your Duty with Detachment:** Arjuna's initial hesitation stemmed from his attachment to the outcomes of his actions. Krishna's counsel helped him understand the importance of performing his duty without attachment to the results.

2. **Seek Wisdom and Guidance:** Arjuna's transformation began with his willingness to seek and accept Krishna's wisdom. By turning to a wise counselor, he gained clarity and strength.

3. **Overcome Fear and Doubt:** Arjuna's journey is marked by his overcoming of fear and doubt, which initially paralyzed him. Through self-reflection and Krishna's guidance, he found the courage to act.

4. **Uphold Righteousness and Integrity:** Throughout the war, Arjuna remained committed to righteousness and integrity, even in the face of immense adversity.

5. **The Path to Self-Discovery:** Arjuna's quest led him to a profound self-discovery and enlightenment, emphasizing the importance of personal growth.

1.(C)

Crafting Strategies:

Drawing from Krishna's Counsel

In the epic tale of the Mahabharata, there exists a pivotal moment when Arjuna, the valiant warrior prince, finds himself on the battlefield of Kurukshetra, torn between his duty as a warrior and the moral dilemmas that plague his conscience. As the opposing armies stand ready for battle, Arjuna is overcome with doubt and despair, questioning the righteousness of the war and the consequences of his actions.

In this moment of crisis, Arjuna turns to his charioteer, none other than Lord Krishna himself, for guidance. Sensing the turmoil in Arjuna's heart, Krishna begins to impart to him the timeless wisdom of the Bhagavad Gita, offering counsel that transcends the boundaries of time and space.

"Draw from the depths of your being, Arjuna," Krishna advises, his voice carrying the weight of eternity. "Find solace in the knowledge that the soul is immortal and that the deeds of the body are but fleeting. Embrace your duty as a warrior, not out of attachment to the fruits of your actions, but out of devotion to the greater good."

As Krishna speaks, Arjuna's doubts begin to fade, replaced by a sense of clarity and purpose. With renewed resolve, he takes up his bow and prepares to face his destiny, guided by the divine wisdom of his charioteer.

Throughout the long and bloody conflict that follows, Arjuna draws strength from Krishna's counsel, his actions guided by the principles of righteousness and dharma. And when the dust finally settles on the battlefield of Kurukshetra, it is Arjuna who emerges victorious, not only in battle but also in the greater struggle to uphold truth and justice in a world plagued by darkness and deceit.

The story of Arjuna and Krishna stands as a testament to the power of divine guidance and the eternal truths that lie at the heart of existence. For in the darkest moments of despair, it is often in drawing from the wisdom of the divine that we find the strength to overcome adversity and fulfill our destinies.

☞Key Lessons

1. **Embrace Your Duty with Detachment:** Arjuna's initial
    hesitation stemmed from his attachment to the outcomes
    of his actions. Krishna's counsel helped him understand
    the importance of performing his duty without
    attachment to the results.

2. **Seek Wisdom and Guidance:** Arjuna's transformation
    began with his willingness to seek and accept Krishna's
    wisdom. By turning to a wise counselor, he gained clarity
    and strength.

3. **Overcome Fear and Doubt:** Arjuna's journey is marked by
    his overcoming of fear and doubt, which initially paralyzed
    him. Through self-reflection and Krishna's guidance, he
    found the courage to act.

4. **Uphold Righteousness and Integrity:** Throughout the war,
    Arjuna remained committed to righteousness and
    integrity, even in the face of immense adversity.

5. **The Path to Self-Discovery:** Arjuna's quest led him to a
    profound self-discovery and enlightenment, emphasizing
    the importance of personal growth.

2.

Competitive Strategy on the Battlefield

In the ancient Indian epic, the Mahabharata, the battlefield serves as a crucible for competitive strategy, where the forces of righteousness and adharma clash in a struggle for supremacy. This essay delves into the realm of competitive strategy on the battlefield, drawing lessons from the assessments, positions, and opportunities seized by key figures such as Bhishma, Drona, Krishna, and Arjuna. Their actions and decisions offer valuable insights into competitive strategy, highlighting the importance of understanding the competition, strategic positioning, and seizing opportunities for victory.

2.(A)

Assessing the Competition:

Analyzing Kaurava and Pandava Forces

In the ancient land of Bharatavarsha, the stage was set for the greatest conflict ever witnessed by mankind – the Kurukshetra War. Two mighty armies, born from the same lineage, stood poised for battle – the Kauravas, led by the ambitious and treacherous Duryodhana, and the Pandavas, guided by the principles of righteousness and duty.

As the sun rose over the battlefield of Kurukshetra, Arjuna, the noble warrior prince of the Pandavas, surveyed the forces arrayed before him. On one side stood the vast army of the Kauravas, their ranks bolstered by powerful allies and seasoned warriors. Despite their numerical superiority, Arjuna's keen eyes detected weaknesses in their formation – gaps in their defenses, divisions in their ranks, and signs of discontent among their troops.

Turning his gaze to his own army, Arjuna felt a swell of pride and determination. Though outnumbered, the Pandavas were not without their own strengths. With the likes of Bhima, Yudhishthira, Nakula, Sahadeva, and countless other heroes at their side, they possessed courage, skill, and unwavering loyalty to their cause.

But as the moment of battle drew near, doubt gnawed at Arjuna's heart. How could he raise his weapons against his own kin, his beloved teachers, and revered elders? How could he shed the blood of those with whom he had grown up, trained, and shared in both joy and sorrow?

It was then that Arjuna turned to his charioteer, Lord Krishna, for guidance. Sensing his friend's turmoil, Krishna spoke words of wisdom that would echo through the ages, urging Arjuna to rise above his doubts and fulfill his duty as a warrior.

"Analyzing the forces before you, Arjuna, consider not just their numbers or their strength in arms, but the righteousness of their cause," Krishna counseled. "Know that in upholding truth and justice, even in the face of seemingly insurmountable odds, you stand on the side of dharma."

With Krishna's words ringing in his ears, Arjuna's resolve was strengthened. Drawing upon his knowledge of strategy and warfare, he devised a plan that would exploit the weaknesses of the Kaurava forces while maximizing the strengths of his own. With skillful maneuvering and unwavering determination, the

Pandavas launched their attack, driving deep into the heart of the enemy ranks.

As the battle raged on, the forces of righteousness clashed with the forces of darkness, each side fighting fiercely for victory. But in the end, it was the Pandavas who emerged triumphant, their victory not just a testament to their prowess in battle, but to their unwavering commitment to truth, justice, and the principles of dharma.

And so, in the aftermath of the great war of Kurukshetra, the story of Arjuna and Krishna stood as a timeless reminder of the power of wisdom, courage, and righteousness to triumph over adversity and usher in a new era of peace and prosperity for all of humanity.

☞ Key Lessons

1. **Analyzing Strengths and Weaknesses:** Arjuna's keen perception on the battlefield allowed him to identify both the strengths and weaknesses of the opposing forces. By noticing gaps in the Kaurava's defenses and divisions within their ranks, he was able to formulate a strategic plan that capitalized on these vulnerabilities.

2. **Balancing Emotion with Duty:** Arjuna's initial hesitation to fight against his kin underscores the emotional challenges

that leaders often face. However, with Krishna's guidance, Arjuna learns to balance his emotions with his duty, ultimately choosing to fulfill his role as a warrior for the greater good.

3. **Righteousness and Integrity:** Krishna's counsel to Arjuna emphasizes the importance of upholding truth and justice. Arjuna's victory was not just a result of his strategic acumen but also his commitment to dharma (righteousness).

4. **Leveraging Team Strengths:** Arjuna's plan utilized the unique strengths of each Pandava, highlighting the importance of recognizing and leveraging the individual abilities of team members. The coordinated effort of the Pandavas, driven by their skills and loyalty, was crucial to their success.

5. **Strategic Innovation:** Arjuna's ability to devise a plan that took advantage of the Kauravas' weaknesses demonstrates the power of strategic innovation. His approach involved skillful maneuvering and adaptability, critical traits in overcoming a numerically superior enemy.

2.(B)

Positioning for Victory

Lessons from Bhishma and Drona

In the vast tapestry of the Mahabharata, two towering figures loom large – Bhishma, the noble patriarch, and Drona, the revered guru. Bound by duty and honor, yet torn by the complexities of human nature, their lives offer profound lessons that resonate through the ages.

Bhishma, the granduncle of both the Pandavas and the Kauravas, was a paragon of virtue and loyalty. Renouncing the throne for the sake of his father's happiness, he swore an oath of celibacy and dedicated his life to serving the kingdom of Hastinapura. Wise and just, Bhishma embodied the ideals of sacrifice and duty, even when it meant standing against those he loved.

Drona, on the other hand, was a master of warfare and the preceptor of both the Pandavas and the Kauravas. Gifted with unparalleled skill in archery and military strategy, he trained princes and warriors alike, molding them into formidable champions of the battlefield. Yet beneath his veneer of honor and discipline lay a heart burdened by ambition and resentment, fueled by a lifetime of unfulfilled desires and thwarted dreams.

As the great war of Kurukshetra loomed on the horizon, Bhishma and Drona found themselves torn between their duties as warriors and their bonds of affection for the Kauravas. Though they knew the righteousness lay with the Pandavas, their loyalty to the throne and their obligations as teachers clouded their judgment, leading them down a path of conflict and tragedy.

In the heat of battle, Bhishma and Drona fought with valor and skill, leading the Kaurava forces with unwavering determination. Yet even as they wielded their weapons with deadly precision, their hearts were heavy with sorrow and regret. For they knew that their actions would bring about the destruction of their own kin, tearing apart the very fabric of their family and kingdom.

As the war reached its climax, Bhishma and Drona found themselves confronted with the consequences of their choices. In a moment of clarity, they realized that true greatness lay not in the pursuit of power or glory, but in the pursuit of righteousness and compassion. With their last breaths, they imparted to their disciples the wisdom they had gleaned from a lifetime of triumphs and tribulations – the importance of upholding dharma above all else, and the value of humility and forgiveness in the face of adversity.

And so, as the dust settled on the battlefield of Kurukshetra, the lessons of Bhishma and Drona echoed through the recorded history, reminding humanity of the eternal truths that guide us on our journey through life – the power of duty, the strength of sacrifice, and the necessity of compassion in a world torn apart by strife and division.

✿❀✿❀✿❀✿❀✿❀✿

☞Key Lessons

1. **The Burden of Unwavering Duty:** Bhishma's life was defined by his unwavering commitment to duty. His vow of celibacy and loyalty to the throne of Hastinapura are testaments to his steadfast dedication. Despite his righteousness, Bhishma's strict adherence to duty often led him to support the Kauravas, even when he knew the Pandavas were on the side of justice.

2. **The Conflict Between Professional and Personal Obligations:** Drona, despite being the revered teacher of both the Pandavas and Kauravas, struggled with personal ambitions and past resentments. His decision to support the Kauravas was driven by a mix of loyalty and his own complex emotions, leading to tragic consequences.

3. **The Importance of Righteousness and Compassion:** In their final moments, both Bhishma and Drona realized that true greatness lies in righteousness and compassion,

not in the pursuit of power. Their regret over the destruction caused by their actions highlights the importance of aligning one's actions with moral and ethical principles.

4. **Balancing Ambition with Ethical Conduct:** Drona's life was marred by unfulfilled ambitions and the resentment that followed. His actions, driven by personal vendettas and ambitions, ultimately led to his downfall.

2.(C)

Seizing Opportunities

Strategies of Krishna and Arjuna

In the grand epic of the Mahabharata, amidst the chaos of war and the clash of mighty armies, there existed a bond of friendship and camaraderie that transcended the boundaries of time and space – the bond between Krishna, the divine charioteer, and Arjuna, the valiant warrior prince.

As the great war of Kurukshetra loomed on the horizon, Arjuna found himself grappling with doubt and despair, torn between his duty as a warrior and the moral dilemmas that plagued his conscience. Sensing his friend's turmoil, Krishna stepped forward to offer guidance, his words carrying the weight of eternity.

"Draw from the depths of your being, Arjuna," Krishna counseled, his voice resonating with wisdom. "Find solace in the knowledge that the soul is immortal and that the deeds of the body are but fleeting. Embrace your duty as a warrior, not out of attachment to the fruits of your actions, but out of devotion to the greater good."

With Krishna's guidance ringing in his ears, Arjuna's resolve was strengthened, and he took up his bow and prepared to face his destiny. But Krishna's role was not limited to mere words of wisdom – he was also a master strategist, guiding Arjuna through the complexities of warfare with unparalleled skill and foresight.

As the battle raged on, Krishna and Arjuna worked together as one, their minds attuned to each other's thoughts and their actions guided by a shared sense of purpose. Through cunning maneuvers and strategic brilliance, they outwitted their foes at every turn, exploiting weaknesses in the enemy's formation and maximizing the strengths of their own forces.

But perhaps their greatest triumph came in the form of the Bhagavad Gita – the timeless discourse on duty and righteousness that Krishna imparted to Arjuna on the battlefield. In those sacred verses, Krishna revealed the secrets of life and death, of action and inaction, laying bare the eternal truths that govern the universe.

With Krishna's guidance and Arjuna's unwavering determination, the Pandavas emerged victorious in the great war of Kurukshetra, their triumph not just a testament to their prowess in battle, but to the power of friendship, wisdom, and devotion to the path of righteousness.

The story of Krishna and Arjuna stands as a timeless reminder of the bond between teacher and student, friend and companion –

a bond forged in the crucible of war and tempered by the fires of adversity yet enduring through the ages as a beacon of hope and inspiration for all of humanity.

☞ Key Lessons

1. **The Power of Guidance and Mentorship:** Krishna's role as a guide and mentor to Arjuna highlights the importance of having a trusted advisor who can provide wisdom and clarity in times of crisis. Krishna's counsel helped Arjuna overcome his doubts and embrace his duty with confidence and resolve.

2. **The Balance of Emotion and Duty:** Arjuna's internal struggle between his emotions and his duty as a warrior reflects a universal human experience. Krishna's teachings helped Arjuna find a balance, enabling him to perform his duties without being overwhelmed by emotional turmoil.

3. **Strategic Thinking and Adaptability:** Krishna's strategic acumen in guiding Arjuna through the complexities of warfare illustrates the importance of strategic thinking and adaptability. Their ability to outmaneuver the enemy was crucial to their success.

4. **The Pursuit of Righteousness and Ethical Conduct:** The Bhagavad Gita's teachings emphasize the importance of

performing one's duty with a focus on righteousness and ethical conduct, rather than being attached to the results of one's actions.

3.

Strategic Maneuvers in the Great War

The Great War of the Mahabharata stands as a timeless testament to the art of strategic maneuvering in the face of adversity. This essay explores key instances of strategic brilliance on the battlefield, focusing on the exploits of three prominent figures: Karna, Arjuna, and Bhima. From exploiting weaknesses and demonstrating adaptability to innovating in warfare, their actions serve as invaluable lessons in strategic thinking and execution. Through a careful examination of their maneuvers, we gain insight into the complexities of warfare and the enduring principles of strategic success.

3.(A)

Exploiting Weaknesses:

Karna's Fatal Flaw

In the epic saga of the Mahabharata, amidst the clash of kingdoms and the trials of heroes, there existed a figure whose fate was as tragic as it was profound – Karna, the illustrious warrior with a fatal flaw that would ultimately seal his destiny.

Born to Kunti, the mother of the Pandavas, and the sun god Surya, Karna was a man of extraordinary talent and boundless courage. Gifted with unparalleled skill in archery and unmatched valor in battle, he rose from humble beginnings to become a formidable rival to even the mightiest of warriors.

But beneath Karna's outward bravado lay a deep-seated insecurity – the knowledge of his lowly birth and the stigma of being raised as a charioteer's son. Despite his many accomplishments, Karna was plagued by a sense of inadequacy and a burning desire for validation and acceptance.

It was this fatal flaw – his relentless pursuit of recognition and respect – that would ultimately lead Karna down a path of tragedy and sorrow. For despite his noble qualities and acts of valor, Karna's allegiance to Duryodhana, the ambitious prince of the Kauravas, blinded him to the righteousness of the Pandavas' cause and the consequences of his actions.

Throughout the great war of Kurukshetra, Karna fought with unmatched ferocity and determination, laying waste to the Pandava forces with his formidable skills and unwavering loyalty to his friend and benefactor, Duryodhana. But as the battle raged on and the tide of war turned against the Kauravas, Karna found himself confronted with the truth of his own folly.

In a moment of clarity, Karna realized the gravity of his mistake – his blind allegiance to Duryodhana had led him astray from the path of righteousness, and his relentless pursuit of honor and recognition had blinded him to the suffering of those around him. With his dying breath, Karna lamented the choices that had led him to this point, his heart heavy with regret and sorrow.

And yet, even in death, Karna's tragic tale serves as a poignant reminder of the dangers of pride and hubris, and the consequences of allowing our insecurities and desires to cloud our judgment. For in the end, it was not Karna's skill in battle or his valor on the battlefield that defined him, but the fatal flaw that lay at the heart of his being – a flaw that would ultimately seal his destiny and leave behind a legacy of sorrow and regret.

☞Key Lessons

1. **The Dangers of Pride and Hubris:** Karna's unyielding pride in his skills and his relentless pursuit of recognition led him to make choices that ultimately sealed his fate. Despite his noble qualities, his hubris often clouded his judgment, pushing him to align with Duryodhana against the Pandavas.

2. **The Consequences of Blind Loyalty:** Karna's loyalty to Duryodhana, though admirable in its steadfastness, ultimately led him to support a cause that was unjust. His inability to question Duryodhana's motives and actions caused him to overlook the righteousness of the Pandavas' cause.

3. **The Struggle for Identity and Validation:** Karna's life was defined by his struggle for identity and validation, stemming from the stigma of his lowly birth and his desire to be recognized as an equal among the Kshatriyas. This pursuit often led him to make compromises that went against his better judgment.

3.(B)

Adaptability in Action

Arjuna's Mastery of Charioteering

In the grand saga of the Mahabharata, amidst the turmoil of war and the clash of mighty warriors, there existed a figure whose mastery of charioteering stood unrivaled – Arjuna, the valiant prince of the Pandavas.

From a young age, Arjuna had shown a natural aptitude for the art of archery and warfare, honing his skills under the tutelage of his divine mentor, Lord Krishna. But it was his mastery of charioteering – the skillful manipulation of horses and chariot in the heat of battle – that truly set him apart as a warrior without equal.

As the charioteer of Arjuna, Krishna guided him through the complexities of combat with unparalleled skill and foresight. Together, they moved as one across the battlefield, their minds attuned to each other's thoughts and their actions guided by a shared sense of purpose.

With swift and nimble movements, Arjuna expertly maneuvered his chariot through the chaos of war, weaving between ranks of soldiers and dodging volleys of arrows with ease. His hands were steady, his aim true, as he unleashed a hail of arrows upon his foes, striking down enemy after enemy with deadly precision.

But perhaps Arjuna's greatest feat of charioteering came during the critical moments of the war, when he faced off against the mighty warrior Karna – his equal in skill and valor. As the two warriors clashed on the battlefield, their chariots raced across the dusty plains, leaving a trail of destruction in their wake.

But whereas Karna relied on brute strength and raw power, Arjuna's mastery of charioteering allowed him to outmaneuver his opponent at every turn, exploiting weaknesses in Karna's defense and striking with precision and finesse. With each passing moment, Arjuna's skill and determination shone brightly, until at last, he emerged victorious, his arrow finding its mark and felling his formidable foe.

The story of Arjuna's mastery of charioteering stands as a testament to the power of skill, discipline, and dedication in the pursuit of greatness. For in the heat of battle, it is not just strength of arms or valor in combat that determines victory, but the mastery of one's craft and the ability to wield it with precision and finesse – qualities that Arjuna possessed in abundance, and which set him apart as one of the greatest warriors of all time.

☞Key Lessons

1. **The Power of Skill and Mastery:** Arjuna's expertise in charioteering and archery set him apart from his peers and enemies. His ability to maneuver his chariot with precision and strike his targets with unfailing accuracy was the result of years of dedicated practice and learning.

2. **The Importance of a Great Mentor:** Arjuna's success was significantly influenced by his divine mentor, Krishna, whose guidance and wisdom were instrumental in shaping his abilities and decisions on the battlefield.

3. **Precision and Finesse Over Raw Power:** Arjuna's victory over Karna highlighted the effectiveness of precision and finesse over brute strength. His strategic thinking and expert maneuvering allowed him to outsmart and outmaneuver his opponent.

4. **Adaptability in the Face of Challenges:** Arjuna's ability to navigate through the chaos of battle, adapt to rapidly changing situations, and exploit his enemy's weaknesses demonstrates the importance of adaptability.

5. **Dedication and Discipline:** Arjuna's dedication to his craft and discipline in practice were fundamental to his achievements. His commitment to continuous learning and improvement was unwavering.

3.(C)

Innovations in Warfare

Bhima's Unconventional Tactics

In the great epic of the Mahabharata, amidst the clash of kingdoms and the trials of heroes, there existed a figure whose unconventional tactics and unmatched strength set him apart on the battlefield – Bhima, the mighty warrior prince of the Pandavas.

Unlike his brother Arjuna, whose mastery of archery and charioteering was renowned throughout the land, Bhima relied on brute strength and sheer force of will to overcome his foes. Towering over his adversaries and possessed of a strength that knew no bounds, Bhima struck fear into the hearts of his enemies and inspired awe in all who beheld him.

But it was not just Bhima's physical prowess that made him a formidable warrior – it was his unconventional tactics and unorthodox methods that truly set him apart on the battlefield. Unlike the disciplined and strategic approach favored by many of his peers, Bhima's fighting style was characterized by its raw power and unpredictability, often catching his foes off guard and leaving them reeling in shock and confusion.

One such instance occurred during the great war of Kurukshetra, when Bhima found himself face to face with Duryodhana, the arrogant prince of the Kauravas. With his superior strength and skill in combat, Duryodhana seemed an unbeatable opponent, his armor impenetrable and his swordsmanship unmatched.

But Bhima, undaunted by the challenge before him, employed an unconventional tactic that would ultimately lead to Duryodhana's downfall. Seizing hold of a mace that lay nearby, Bhima engaged Duryodhana in a fierce duel, his blows raining down upon his opponent with relentless fury.

With each swing of his weapon, Bhima battered away at Duryodhana's defenses, slowly but surely wearing him down with the sheer force of his onslaught. And when at last, Duryodhana's strength began to wane and his defenses faltered, Bhima delivered the final blow, striking his opponent down with a mighty blow that echoed across the battlefield.

In the aftermath of the battle, Bhima's unconventional tactics and unmatched strength earned him the admiration and respect of friend and foe alike. For in a world where victory often went to the cunning and the strategic, Bhima's raw power and unwavering determination stood as a testament to the indomitable spirit of the human soul – a spirit that knows no bounds and refuses to be bound by convention or tradition.

☞Key Lessons

1. **Harnessing Unique Strengths:** Bhima's unmatched physical prowess was his greatest asset on the battlefield. Unlike his brother Arjuna, who relied on skill and precision, Bhima leveraged his brute strength to overpower his enemies.

2. **Embracing Unconventional Tactics:** Bhima's success often came from his unconventional and unpredictable methods. His ability to think outside the box and use unexpected strategies gave him an edge over his opponents.

3. **Relentless Determination:** Bhima's relentless pursuit and unwavering determination were crucial in his victories. His refusal to back down, even against formidable opponents like Duryodhana, demonstrated his indomitable spirit.

4. **Adapting to the Situation:** Bhima's ability to adapt his tactics based on the situation at hand was instrumental in his success. He used the mace against Duryodhana, understanding that brute force would be more effective than conventional weapons.

5. **Inspiring Through Action:** Bhima's actions on the battlefield inspired admiration and respect from both allies and enemies. His courage and strength served as a powerful example of what can be achieved through sheer willpower and bravery.

4.

Resource Allocation and Management

Resource allocation and management are critical aspects of any endeavor, particularly in the context of war where the efficient use of resources can often determine the outcome of battles. This essay delves into the Mahabharata, drawing valuable lessons from the resource management strategies employed by key figures. From Yudhishthira's meticulous organization of his army to the Pandava's effective logistics and supply chain operations, and even exploring the ethical dimensions of wealth distribution as exemplified by the concept of Dharma, this examination sheds light on the principles and practices of resource allocation in challenging environments. Through these insights, we can glean timeless wisdom that is applicable not only to military campaigns but also to various aspects of life where resource management is crucial.

4.(A)

Mobilizing Forces:

Yudhishthira's Army Organization

In the grand saga of the Mahabharata, amidst the tumult of war and the clash of kingdoms, there existed a figure whose strategic acumen and organizational skills were instrumental in shaping the fate of nations – Yudhishthira, the wise and noble eldest prince of the Pandavas.

As the great war of Kurukshetra loomed on the horizon, Yudhishthira faced the daunting task of organizing and leading his army into battle against the formidable forces of the Kauravas. With the lives of countless warriors hanging in the balance, Yudhishthira knew that the key to victory lay not just in strength of arms, but in careful planning and meticulous organization.

Drawing upon his years of experience as a prince and a leader, Yudhishthira set about assembling his army with precision and foresight. He divided his forces into various units, each with its own specialized role and complement of warriors, ensuring that every aspect of warfare was covered and accounted for.

At the forefront of his army stood the vanguard — a select group of elite warriors renowned for their skill and valor in combat. Led by the likes of Bhima, Arjuna, and other renowned heroes, the vanguard served as the spearhead of Yudhishthira's forces, striking fear into the hearts of their enemies and leading the charge into battle.

Behind the vanguard marched the infantry — a vast array of foot soldiers armed with swords, spears, and shields. Trained to fight in close quarters and withstand the onslaught of enemy forces, the infantry formed the backbone of Yudhishthira's army, holding the line against wave after wave of enemy attacks.

Supporting the infantry were the archers — skilled marksmen armed with bows and arrows, capable of raining down death upon their foes from a distance. Positioned strategically behind the front lines, the archers provided cover and support for their comrades, picking off enemy soldiers with deadly accuracy and precision.

And finally, there were the charioteers and cavalry — swift and agile warriors mounted on horseback or driving chariots into battle. With their speed and mobility, they were able to outmaneuver their foes on the battlefield, striking swiftly and decisively when the moment was right.

Together, under Yudhishthira's wise and steady leadership, these diverse units formed a cohesive and formidable fighting force — an army united in purpose and determined to uphold the principles of righteousness and justice. And as they marched forth to meet their destiny on the battlefield of Kurukshetra, they did so with courage in their hearts and faith in their leader, knowing that victory would be theirs as long as they stood united against the forces of darkness.

☞Key Lessons

1. **Importance of Strategic Planning:** Yudhishthira's meticulous planning and foresight were crucial in organizing the Pandava army. He understood that victory depended not only on the might of individual warriors but on the strategic deployment of his forces.

2. **Effective Division of Labor:** Yudhishthira divided his forces into specialized units — vanguard, infantry, archers, and charioteers — each with a specific role, ensuring that every aspect of warfare was covered.

3. **Leadership and Trust:** Yudhishthira's leadership inspired trust and unity among his troops. His wisdom and steady guidance gave his warriors confidence and a clear sense of purpose.

4. **Adaptability and Flexibility:** Yudhishthira's forces were composed of diverse units, each capable of adapting to

different combat situations. This flexibility allowed them to respond effectively to various challenges on the battlefield.

5. **Unity and Teamwork:** Yudhishthira's ability to unite diverse warriors under a common cause highlights the importance of teamwork. His leadership ensured that each unit worked in harmony towards their shared objective.

6. **Moral Leadership:** Yudhishthira's leadership was rooted in righteousness and justice. His commitment to dharma (moral duty) guided his actions and decisions, earning him the respect and loyalty of his followers.

4.(B)

Logistics and Supply Chains

Insights from Pandava Camp Operations

In the sprawling encampment of the Pandavas, amidst the rustle of canvas tents and the clatter of armor, there existed a hive of activity and strategic planning that would shape the outcome of the great war of Kurukshetra. Here, within the confines of their makeshift headquarters, the five brothers and their allies gathered to discuss tactics, assess their strengths and weaknesses, and prepare for the inevitable clash with the forces of the Kauravas.

Led by Yudhishthira, the eldest of the Pandavas and a master strategist in his own right, the camp operations ran with precision and efficiency, each aspect carefully coordinated to maximize their chances of victory on the battlefield. From the allocation of resources to the training of troops, every decision was made with careful consideration and foresight.

At the heart of the Pandava camp lay a council of war – a gathering of the most seasoned commanders and advisors, each offering their insights and expertise to help guide the brothers in their quest for victory. Among them were Bhishma, the venerable patriarch of the Kuru dynasty, and Drona, the revered guru and preceptor of both the Pandavas and the Kauravas.

Together, they pored over maps and battle plans, analyzing the strengths and weaknesses of their own forces and those of their enemies. They discussed strategies for engaging the Kaurava forces, debating the merits of frontal assaults versus guerrilla tactics, and weighing the risks and rewards of various maneuvers on the battlefield.

But perhaps the most valuable insights came from within the ranks of the Pandava brothers themselves – each bringing their own unique perspective and skills to the table. Arjuna, with his mastery of archery and charioteering, offered strategies for exploiting weaknesses in the enemy's formation and maximizing the effectiveness of their own forces. Bhima, with his unmatched strength and valor, proposed daring and unconventional tactics that took their foes by surprise and turned the tide of battle in their favor. Nakula and Sahadeva, with their keen intellects and knowledge of military strategy, provided invaluable insights into the movements and motivations of their adversaries, helping to anticipate their next moves and stay one step ahead.

And through it all, Yudhishthira stood as a beacon of wisdom and guidance, his calm demeanor and unwavering resolve inspiring confidence in his comrades and allies. With his steady hand at the helm, the Pandava camp operations ran smoothly and efficiently, each decision made with the utmost care and consideration for the lives of their soldiers and the fate of their kingdom.

As the hour of battle drew near, the Pandava brothers and their allies stood united in purpose and resolve, ready to face whatever challenges lay ahead. For they knew that victory would not come easily, but with careful planning, steadfast determination, and the insights gleaned from their camp operations, they stood poised to emerge triumphant in the struggle for righteousness and justice.

☞Key Lessons

1. **Strategic Planning and Coordination:** The success of the Pandavas was largely due to their meticulous planning and strategic coordination. Every aspect, from resource allocation to troop training, was carefully considered to ensure maximum efficiency and effectiveness on the battlefield.

2. **Leveraging Expertise and Diverse Perspectives:** The council of war in the Pandava camp included seasoned commanders and advisors who brought diverse perspectives and expertise to the table. This collective

wisdom helped in devising effective strategies and making informed decisions.

3. **Adaptability and Unconventional Tactics:** Bhima's proposal of daring and unconventional tactics illustrates the importance of being adaptable and willing to think outside the box. Such tactics can surprise adversaries and turn the tide in one's favor.

4. **Leadership and Unity:** Yudhishthira's calm demeanor and unwavering resolve as a leader inspired confidence and unity among the Pandava brothers and their allies. Effective leadership involves guiding with wisdom, fostering collaboration, and maintaining morale.

5. **Anticipating and Preempting Opponents' Moves:** Nakula and Sahadeva's keen intellects and strategic insights into the enemy's movements allowed the Pandavas to anticipate and stay ahead of their adversaries.

4.(C)

Wealth Distribution

Dharma's Ethical Resource Allocation

In the epic tale of the Mahabharata, amidst the tumult of war and the clash of kingdoms, there existed a figure whose commitment to dharma – righteousness and duty – guided his every action, even in the face of seemingly insurmountable challenges. This figure was none other than Yudhishthira, the noble and virtuous eldest prince of the Pandavas.

As the Pandavas prepared for the great war of Kurukshetra, Yudhishthira faced the daunting task of allocating their limited resources – weapons, provisions, and manpower – in a manner that would maximize their chances of victory while upholding the principles of dharma. With the lives of countless warriors hanging in the balance, Yudhishthira knew that every decision he made would carry grave consequences.

Drawing upon his deep sense of ethics and his unwavering commitment to righteousness, Yudhishthira set about the task with diligence and care. He convened a council of wise advisors and seasoned commanders, seeking their counsel and expertise in matters of strategy and resource allocation.

Together, they assessed the strengths and weaknesses of their own forces and those of their enemies, analyzing the available resources and formulating a plan that would allow them to make the most efficient use of their limited assets. Weapons and armor were distributed according to need, with priority given to those warriors whose skills and valor would be most instrumental in securing victory on the battlefield.

But Yudhishthira's commitment to dharma went beyond mere logistics – it extended to every aspect of the Pandava war effort, from the treatment of prisoners of war to the care of wounded soldiers. He ensured that captured enemies were treated with dignity and respect, offering them the chance to surrender and join their cause if they so wished. He also established hospitals and medical tents where wounded warriors could receive treatment and care, regardless of their allegiance or background.

Through it all, Yudhishthira remained steadfast in his adherence to dharma, never wavering in his commitment to uphold the principles of righteousness and justice, even in the face of adversity. And though the path ahead was fraught with peril and uncertainty, he faced the challenges with courage and conviction, secure in the knowledge that his actions were guided by the highest ideals of morality and ethics.

As the great war of Kurukshetra unfolded, Yudhishthira's ethical resource allocation proved to be a crucial factor in the Pandavas' eventual victory. For in the end, it was not just their skill in battle or their valor on the battlefield that determined their triumph, but their unwavering commitment to dharma – a commitment that guided their every action and ensured the righteousness of their cause prevailed in the end.

☞ Key Lessons

1. **Ethical Leadership and Decision-Making:** Yudhishthira's leadership was characterized by his unwavering commitment to dharma. He consistently made decisions based on ethical considerations, ensuring that every action was aligned with the principles of righteousness.

2. **Strategic Resource Allocation:** Yudhishthira's careful allocation of limited resources demonstrates the importance of strategic planning and prioritization. By assessing strengths, weaknesses, and needs, he ensured that resources were used efficiently to maximize their impact.

3. **Inclusivity and Compassion in Warfare:** Yudhishthira's humane treatment of prisoners of war and the care provided to wounded soldiers highlight his commitment

to compassion and inclusivity, even amidst conflict.

4. **Consultative Decision-Making:** Yudhishthira's practice of convening a council of advisors and commanders to seek their counsel underscores the value of collaborative and consultative decision-making.

5. **Commitment to Moral Principles:** Throughout the Mahabharata, Yudhishthira's adherence to dharma, even in challenging circumstances, serves as a reminder of the importance of staying true to one's moral principles.

5. Motivation and Energy Management

Motivation and energy management are fundamental to achieving success in any endeavor, particularly in times of adversity and challenge. In the epic of the Mahabharata, we find rich examples of individuals who exemplified extraordinary motivation and energy management techniques. From Krishna's charismatic leadership that inspired unwavering devotion to Draupadi's resilience in the face of humiliation and the Pandavas' endurance during their exile, these stories offer profound insights into the human spirit's capacity to overcome obstacles. By exploring these narratives, we can glean valuable lessons on how to cultivate motivation, manage energy effectively, and navigate through life's trials with resilience and determination.

5.(A)

Inspiring Devotion

Krishna's Leadership Style

In the grand saga of the Mahabharata, amidst the chaos of war and the clash of kingdoms, there existed a leader whose wisdom, compassion, and unwavering guidance were instrumental in shaping the destiny of nations – Krishna, the divine charioteer and counselor of the Pandavas.

As the great war of Kurukshetra loomed on the horizon, Krishna found himself thrust into a pivotal role as the leader and mentor of the Pandava brothers. With his unmatched wisdom and foresight, he guided them through the trials and tribulations of war, offering counsel and support in their darkest hours.

Krishna's leadership style was characterized by its compassion and empathy, tempered by a firm commitment to righteousness and justice. He listened to the concerns and grievances of his comrades with an open heart, offering words of comfort and encouragement to those in need. Yet, when the situation demanded it, he could also be stern and uncompromising in his resolve to uphold dharma – the principles of righteousness and duty.

One of Krishna's greatest strengths as a leader lay in his ability to inspire others to greatness. With his words of wisdom and his unwavering faith in their abilities, he instilled confidence and courage in the hearts of his comrades, motivating them to rise above their fears and doubts and embrace their destinies as warriors.

But perhaps Krishna's most enduring legacy as a leader was his unwavering commitment to the greater good. Throughout the war of Kurukshetra, he worked tirelessly to ensure that the Pandavas' cause was just and their actions were guided by the highest ideals of morality and ethics. He sought to minimize the loss of life wherever possible, offering his enemies the chance to surrender and join their cause, and extending compassion and mercy to all who crossed his path.

And when the time came for decisive action, Krishna did not hesitate to take matters into his own hands, leading by example and showing his comrades the way forward with his fearless courage and unyielding determination.

Krishna's leadership style stands as a timeless example of the qualities that define a true leader – wisdom, compassion, integrity, and a steadfast commitment to the greater good. Through his guidance and example, he inspired generations of leaders to come, reminding them that true greatness lies not in power or prestige, but in service to others and the pursuit of righteousness and justice.

☞ Key Lessons

1. **Compassionate Leadership:** Krishna's leadership was characterized by compassion and empathy. He listened to the concerns of others, offering comfort and encouragement when needed. His ability to connect with people on an emotional level strengthened his relationships and inspired loyalty.

2. **Wisdom and Foresight:** Krishna's wisdom and foresight allowed him to see the bigger picture and make decisions that were in the best interest of all. His strategic thinking and ability to anticipate outcomes were instrumental in guiding the Pandavas through the challenges they faced.

3. **Commitment to Dharma:** Krishna's commitment to dharma, or righteousness, guided his actions and decisions. He upheld moral and ethical principles, even in the midst of conflict, setting a powerful example for others to follow.

4. **Inspiring Others:** Krishna's ability to inspire greatness in others was a key aspect of his leadership. His words of encouragement and unwavering faith in his comrades motivated them to rise above their fears and doubts.

5. **Service-Oriented Leadership:** Krishna's leadership was driven by a desire to serve the greater good. He worked tirelessly to ensure that the Pandavas' cause was just and that their actions were guided by morality and ethics.

5.(B)

Overcoming Adversity:

Draupadi's Resilience

In the vast epic of the Mahabharata, amidst the tumult of war and the clash of kingdoms, there existed a figure whose resilience and strength of spirit served as a beacon of hope in the darkest of times – Draupadi, the noble and steadfast wife of the Pandavas.

From her humble beginnings as the daughter of King Drupada to her eventual role as the queen of the Pandavas, Draupadi's life was marked by trials and tribulations that would test the very limits of her endurance. Yet through it all, she remained unwavering in her resolve, drawing upon her inner strength and determination to overcome every obstacle in her path.

One of Draupadi's greatest challenges came during the infamous game of dice, where her husband Yudhishthira wagered and lost her in a game of chance to the Kauravas. Humiliated and stripped of her dignity, Draupadi found herself at the mercy of her enemies, subjected to insults and abuse in full view of the court.

But even in the face of such adversity, Draupadi refused to be broken. With fiery defiance in her eyes, she confronted her tormentors, challenging them to justify their actions and demanding justice for the injustice that had been done to her. Though her voice trembled with anger and grief, her spirit remained unbroken, a testament to her resilience and strength of character.

As the situation grew increasingly dire, Draupadi turned to her husbands for support, calling upon them to defend her honor and uphold their duty as warriors and princes. And though they were powerless to change the outcome of the game, they stood by her side, offering words of comfort and reassurance in her darkest hour.

But perhaps Draupadi's greatest act of resilience came in the aftermath of the game of dice, when she vowed to seek vengeance against her enemies and reclaim her rightful place as queen of the Pandavas. With steely determination and unwavering resolve, she set about plotting her revenge, biding her time until the moment was right to strike back against those who had wronged her.

And when the time came for the great war of Kurukshetra, Draupadi stood shoulder to shoulder with her husbands on the battlefield, a symbol of strength and resilience in the face of adversity. Though she wielded no weapons and wore no armor, her presence alone inspired courage and determination in her comrades, driving them forward in their quest for justice and righteousness.

Draupadi's resilience stands as a timeless example of the power of the human spirit to overcome even the greatest of challenges. Through her unwavering courage and determination, she proved that no obstacle is insurmountable, and that true strength lies not in physical prowess, but in the resilience of the human heart.

☞Key Lessons

1. **Courage in the Face of Adversity:** Draupadi faced numerous challenges throughout her life, yet she never wavered in her resolve. Her courage in standing up to injustice, even when faced with humiliation and abuse, teaches us the importance of standing firm in our beliefs and principles.

2. **Resilience in Times of Crisis:** Despite the hardships she faced, Draupadi remained resilient, refusing to be broken by the trials of life. Her ability to bounce back from adversity and maintain her strength of spirit serves as a powerful example of resilience.

3. **Seeking Justice with Determination:** Draupadi's quest for justice after the game of dice demonstrates her unwavering determination to right the wrongs done to her. Her

commitment to seeking justice serves as a reminder of the importance of standing up against injustice.

4. **Strength in Unity:** Throughout her trials, Draupadi found strength in her relationships with her husbands and allies. Their support and solidarity were crucial in helping her navigate the challenges she faced.

5. **Inspiring Others with Resilience:** Draupadi's unwavering spirit inspired those around her, rallying them to her cause and motivating them to fight for justice. Her resilience serves as a beacon of hope and inspiration for others facing difficult circumstances.

5.(C)

Endurance and Resilience

Lessons from the Pandavas' Exile

In the epic tale of the Mahabharata, amidst the intrigue of court politics and the rivalry of royal families, there existed a period of exile that tested the endurance and resilience of the Pandavas – the noble and valiant princes banished from their kingdom by the machinations of their cousins, the Kauravas.

The story began with a game of dice, a seemingly innocent pastime that quickly spiraled into a tragic turn of events. Yudhishthira, the eldest of the Pandavas, found himself drawn into a high-stakes game against the Kauravas, with disastrous consequences. Through deceit and trickery, the Pandavas lost everything – their wealth, their kingdom, and even their freedom.

Forced to relinquish their claim to the throne, the Pandavas were exiled from their kingdom for thirteen long years, with an additional year spent incognito. With heavy hearts and determination in their souls, they set out into the wilderness, accompanied by their faithful wife Draupadi.

The years of exile were a time of hardship and trial for the Pandavas, as they roamed the forests and mountains, living off the land and facing countless dangers along the way. Yet through it all, they remained united in their determination to reclaim their rightful kingdom and restore their honor.

During their time in exile, the Pandavas encountered many challenges and adversaries, from fierce demons and wild beasts to jealous rivals and treacherous foes. But with courage and resourcefulness, they overcame every obstacle that stood in their path, proving themselves worthy of the throne they had been denied.

Yet perhaps the greatest trial of all came in the final year of their exile, when they were forced to live in hiding, disguised as common travelers to avoid detection by their enemies. It was during this time that they faced their most difficult tests of character and resolve, as they struggled to maintain their dignity and honor in the face of adversity.

But through it all, the Pandavas remained steadfast in their commitment to righteousness and justice, drawing strength from each other and from their unwavering faith in the divine. And when the time came for them to return to their kingdom and claim their birthright, they did so with heads held high and hearts filled with hope for a brighter future.

The story of the Pandavas' exile stands as a testament to the power of resilience and determination in the face of adversity. Through their trials and tribulations, they proved themselves to be true heroes – not just in the eyes of men, but in the eyes of the gods themselves. And though their journey was long and arduous, it ultimately led them to victory and glory, as they reclaimed their kingdom and restored peace and prosperity to their land.

☞Key Lessons

1. **Resilience in the Face of Adversity:** The Pandavas' exile was a period of immense hardship, yet they remained resilient and determined throughout. Their ability to endure challenges and persevere in the face of adversity is a testament to the power of resilience.

2. **Unity and Support in Times of Need:** Throughout their exile, the Pandavas remained united and supported each other. Their bond of brotherhood and their unwavering support for one another helped them overcome the challenges they faced.

3. **Courage and Determination in Pursuit of Goals:** Despite the hardships they faced, the Pandavas remained determined to reclaim their kingdom and honor. Their

courage and determination in pursuing their goals serve as an inspiration to persevere in the face of challenges.

4. **Adapting to Change and Embracing Challenges:** During their exile, the Pandavas had to adapt to a life of hardship and uncertainty. They embraced the challenges they faced and learned to thrive in difficult circumstances.

5. **Faith and Belief in a Higher Purpose:** Throughout their exile, the Pandavas maintained their faith and belief in a higher purpose. Their unwavering belief in righteousness and justice guided their actions and gave them strength in difficult times.

6. Identifying Strengths and Weaknesses

In the epic Mahabharata, the characters' strengths and weaknesses play a pivotal role in shaping their destinies. This theme resonates deeply, offering timeless lessons on the importance of self-assessment, leveraging strengths, and acknowledging limitations. Yudhishthira's quest for self-realization serves as a poignant example of the power of introspection, highlighting the need to understand one's strengths and weaknesses. The Pandavas, on the other hand, demonstrate the value of embracing each other's abilities, showcasing the importance of teamwork and collaboration in overcoming challenges. Conversely, Duryodhana's fatal flaw lies in his arrogance and refusal to acknowledge his limitations, ultimately leading to his downfall. By examining these narratives, we can gain valuable insights into the significance of identifying strengths and weaknesses, both in ourselves and in others, and the impact this awareness can have on our lives.

6.(A)

Self-Assessment

Yudhishthira's Quest for Self-Realization

In the grand tapestry of the Mahabharata, amidst the tumult of war and the clash of kingdoms, there existed a figure whose quest for self-realization and enlightenment led him on a journey of introspection and discovery – Yudhishthira, the noble and righteous eldest prince of the Pandavas.

From his earliest days, Yudhishthira had been raised in the ways of dharma – righteousness and duty – instilled with a deep sense of honor and integrity by his mother Kunti and his wise uncle Vidura. Yet, despite his unwavering commitment to upholding the principles of righteousness, Yudhishthira found himself grappling with doubts and uncertainties as he faced the trials and tribulations of life.

It was during the great war of Kurukshetra that Yudhishthira's quest for self-realization truly began in earnest. As the Pandavas prepared for battle against their cousins, the Kauravas, Yudhishthira found himself confronted with the harsh realities of war and the weight of leadership upon his shoulders. He questioned the righteousness of his cause and the necessity of shedding blood in the name of duty, struggling to reconcile the teachings of dharma with the brutal realities of warfare.

But it was not until the aftermath of the war, amidst the ruins of the battlefield and the ashes of fallen warriors, that Yudhishthira's quest for self-realization reached its zenith. As he surveyed the carnage and destruction that surrounded him, he was filled with a profound sense of sorrow and remorse, questioning the cost of victory and the price of power.

In that moment of introspection, Yudhishthira realized that true self-realization could not be found in the pursuit of worldly success or the trappings of wealth and power. It lay instead in the cultivation of inner peace and harmony, in the renunciation of attachment and desire, and in the acceptance of life's inevitable cycles of birth, death, and rebirth.

With this newfound understanding, Yudhishthira embarked on a journey of self-discovery, seeking wisdom and enlightenment from sages and ascetics, and delving deep into the mysteries of the soul. He learned to let go of his attachments and desires, and to embrace the impermanence of life with equanimity and grace.

And in the end, Yudhishthira found the true meaning of dharma – not as a set of rigid rules and obligations, but as a path to self-realization and enlightenment, leading him to a state of inner peace and fulfillment that transcended the trials and tribulations of mortal existence.

The story of Yudhishthira's quest for self-realization stands as a timeless reminder of the power of introspection and self-discovery in the pursuit of spiritual enlightenment. Through his journey of self-realization, Yudhishthira found not just the answers to his own questions, but a deeper understanding of the nature of existence itself – a realization that would guide him on the path to true fulfillment and inner peace.

☞ Key Lessons

1. **Questioning and Doubt:** Yudhishthira's journey began with questioning the righteousness of his cause and the nature of duty in the face of war. His willingness to question and doubt reflects the importance of critical thinking and introspection in the search for truth and meaning.

2. **Acceptance of Impermanence:** Through his experiences, Yudhishthira learned to accept the impermanence of life and the inevitability of change. This acceptance allowed him to find inner peace and equanimity amidst the turmoil of war and loss.

3. **Renunciation and Detachment:** Yudhishthira's quest for self-realization led him to renounce attachment to worldly desires and possessions. By letting go of his attachments,

he was able to find inner peace and freedom from suffering.

4. **Seeking Wisdom from Others:** Yudhishthira sought wisdom and enlightenment from sages and ascetics, recognizing the value of learning from others in his quest for self-discovery.

5. **The True Meaning of Dharma:** Through his journey, Yudhishthira came to understand that dharma is not just about following rules and obligations, but about the pursuit of self-realization and spiritual enlightenment.

6.(B)

Leveraging Strengths

Pandavas' Embrace of Each Other's Abilities

In the vast tapestry of the Mahabharata, amidst the trials and tribulations of the Pandavas, there existed a bond of brotherhood that transcended the boundaries of blood and lineage – a bond forged in the crucible of adversity and strengthened by the diversity of their abilities and talents.

From the outset, the Pandavas were a band of brothers united by their shared experiences and their unwavering commitment to righteousness and justice. Each possessed their own unique strengths and abilities, from Arjuna's mastery of archery to Bhima's unmatched strength, Nakula and Sahadeva's knowledge of strategy and diplomacy, and Yudhishthira's wisdom and sense of duty.

But it was not just their individual abilities that set them apart – it was their willingness to embrace and celebrate each other's talents, recognizing that their differences were what made them stronger as a team.

From their earliest days in Hastinapura, the Pandavas learned to rely on each other's strengths and abilities, pooling their resources and working together to overcome the challenges that lay before them. Whether it was navigating the intricacies of court politics or facing off against formidable foes on the battlefield, they stood united as one, each contributing their own unique skills and talents to the greater good.

One of the most striking examples of the Pandavas' embrace of each other's abilities came during their years of exile in the forest. Far from the comforts of their royal palace, they faced countless trials and tribulations, from fierce demons and wild beasts to jealous rivals and treacherous foes. But through it all, they stood together, drawing strength from each other's courage and determination.

Arjuna's skill with the bow and arrow proved invaluable in defending the camp against marauding bandits and wild animals, while Bhima's unmatched strength and ferocity struck fear into the hearts of their enemies. Nakula and Sahadeva's knowledge of the wilderness helped them navigate the treacherous terrain and find food and shelter for their comrades, while Yudhishthira's wisdom and sense of duty guided them through the darkest moments of their journey.

But perhaps the greatest testament to the Pandavas' embrace of each other's abilities came during the great war of Kurukshetra, when they faced off against their cousins, the Kauravas, in a battle for the fate of the kingdom. Though each brother possessed their own unique talents and skills, they fought not as individuals, but as a united front, drawing strength from their bond of brotherhood and their shared commitment to righteousness and justice.

In the end, it was this unity of purpose and diversity of abilities that led the Pandavas to victory, as they stood triumphant on the battlefield, their bond of brotherhood unbroken and their legacy as heroes of legend secure for all time. And though the pages of history may fade and the memories of their deeds may dim, the story of the Pandavas' embrace of each other's abilities will endure as a timeless reminder of the power of unity, diversity, and brotherhood in the face of adversity.

☞Key Lessons

1. **Celebrating Diversity:** The Pandavas' bond was strengthened by their diverse abilities and talents. They recognized that each brother had unique strengths that contributed to the group's success. This teaches us the importance of celebrating diversity and valuing the unique qualities that each individual brings to a team or group.

2. **Unity in Adversity:** Throughout their trials and tribulations, the Pandavas remained united as a team. They faced

challenges together, drawing strength from each other's courage and determination. This demonstrates the power of unity in overcoming adversity.

3. **Pooling Resources:** The Pandavas pooled their resources and worked together to overcome challenges. Each brother contributed their unique skills and talents, recognizing that their collective effort was more powerful than individual actions.

4. **Leading by Example:** The Pandavas led by example, demonstrating the importance of leadership that inspires and motivates others. Each brother's actions and words served as a source of inspiration for the rest of the group.

5. **Staying United in Purpose:** Despite their individual differences, the Pandavas remained united in their purpose and commitment to righteousness and justice. This shared goal served as a guiding principle that kept them focused and determined in the face of challenges.

Acknowledging Limitations

Duryodhana's Fatal Arrogance

In the grand epic of the Mahabharata, amidst the clash of kingdoms and the struggle for power, there existed a figure whose fatal flaw of arrogance would ultimately seal his fate – Duryodhana, the proud and ambitious prince of the Kauravas.

From a young age, Duryodhana's ambition burned brightly, driving him to seek power and prestige at any cost. Fueled by envy and resentment towards his cousins, the Pandavas, he harbored a deep-seated desire to surpass them and claim the throne of Hastinapura for himself.

But it was Duryodhana's arrogance – his unwavering belief in his own superiority and his disregard for the consequences of his actions – that would ultimately lead to his downfall.

From the outset, Duryodhana's arrogance blinded him to the wisdom of his advisors and the warnings of his well-wishers. He dismissed the counsel of his wise uncle Vidura, who urged him to seek reconciliation with the Pandavas and avoid the path of conflict and bloodshed. Instead, he surrounded himself with sycophants and flatterers who fed his ego and reinforced his belief in his own invincibility.

As the rivalry between the Pandavas and the Kauravas escalated, Duryodhana's arrogance only grew more pronounced. He reveled in his wealth and power, flaunting his superiority over his cousins at every opportunity and dismissing their rightful claims to the throne with disdain.

But it was during the game of dice — a fateful contest that would change the course of history — that Duryodhana's arrogance reached its peak. Blinded by his desire for victory and his contempt for the Pandavas, he wagered everything he possessed, including the honor of his wife Draupadi, in a high-stakes game against his cousins.

In his arrogance, Duryodhana believed that he could never lose — that victory was his by divine right and that the rules of dharma did not apply to him. But his arrogance proved to be his undoing, as the game descended into chaos and Draupadi was subjected to unspeakable humiliation at the hands of his cousins.

In the aftermath of the game of dice, Duryodhana's arrogance turned to bitterness and rage, fueling his desire for vengeance against the Pandavas and driving him to the brink of war. Blinded by his own pride and hubris, he refused to heed the warnings of his elders and the pleas of his well-wishers, choosing instead to pursue his own selfish ambitions at any cost.

And in the end, it was Duryodhana's fatal arrogance that led to his downfall, as he faced off against the Pandavas on the battlefield of Kurukshetra and met his end in a final, tragic confrontation. In his arrogance, he had sown the seeds of his own destruction, leaving behind a legacy of pride and folly that would be remembered for generations to come.

☞Key Lessons

1. **Blindness to Wise Counsel:** Duryodhana's arrogance prevented him from listening to the wise counsel of his uncle Vidura, who warned him against his actions. This teaches us the importance of humility in accepting advice and guidance from those who have our best interests at heart.

2. **Overestimation of Abilities:** Duryodhana's arrogance led him to overestimate his own abilities and underestimate his opponents, particularly the Pandavas. This false sense of superiority blinded him to the realities of his situation and clouded his judgment.

3. **Disregard for Consequences:** Duryodhana's arrogance made him disregard the consequences of his actions, leading him to make decisions that had far-reaching and disastrous effects. This teaches us the importance of

considering the potential outcomes of our choices before acting.

4. **Lack of Empathy:** Duryodhana's arrogance made him incapable of empathy towards others, as seen in his treatment of Draupadi during the game of dice. This lack of empathy blinded him to the suffering of others and contributed to his downfall.

5. **Self-Destruction:** Ultimately, Duryodhana's arrogance led to his own downfall. His refusal to heed warnings and his relentless pursuit of power and prestige at any cost led to his defeat and death in the war of Kurukshetra.

7. Adaptive Strategy in Changing Circumstances

In the epic Mahabharata, the ability to adapt to changing circumstances emerges as a crucial theme that determines the fate of kingdoms and individuals alike. The Pandavas, faced with numerous challenges posed by the Kauravas, exhibit a remarkable flexibility in their tactics, constantly adjusting their strategies to navigate the ever-changing battlefield. Their ability to learn from their mistakes and evolve their approach in response to new challenges serves as a valuable lesson in adaptive strategy.

Conversely, the Kauravas' failure to adapt and learn from their missteps ultimately leads to their downfall. Their rigid adherence to flawed strategies and refusal to change course despite mounting evidence of their failures highlights the dangers of inflexibility in the face of changing circumstances.

Amidst this backdrop, Krishna emerges as a beacon of wisdom, offering guidance that emphasizes the importance of agility in decision-making. His ability to provide timely counsel and steer the Pandavas through crisis situations underscores the value of adaptability and quick thinking in navigating complex and dynamic environments. Through an exploration of these narratives, we can glean valuable insights into the principles of adaptive strategy and their relevance in modern-day challenges.

7.(A)

Flexibility in Tactics

Pandavas' Response to Kaurava Challenges

Once upon a time, in the ancient land of Bharat, there lived two great families, the Pandavas and the Kauravas. Bound by blood but divided by destiny, their story is etched in the archive of history as the Mahabharata, a tale of honor, duty, and the eternal struggle between righteousness and greed.

As the rivalry between the Pandavas and the Kauravas escalated, fueled by jealousy and ambition, the Kauravas devised a series of challenges to subdue their cousins. These challenges were not mere games but tests of strength, skill, and courage. Yet, the Pandavas, guided by virtue and integrity, faced each challenge with unwavering determination.

The first challenge came in the form of a mighty competition of archery. The Kauravas, led by the skilled warrior Duryodhana, boasted of their prowess with the bow and arrow. But Arjuna, the greatest archer of his time and the third Pandava, accepted the challenge without hesitation. With Krishna as his charioteer and mentor, Arjuna showcased his unmatched skill, piercing targets with precision and grace. In the end, it was Arjuna's arrows that soared high, leaving the Kauravas in awe of his talent.

Not content with their defeat, the Kauravas devised a more perilous challenge — a duel of maces. Bhima, the second Pandava and a formidable warrior known for his strength, stepped forward to face this trial. His opponent was Duryodhana himself, fueled by his desire to prove his superiority. The clash of their maces echoed through the battlefield as Bhima's raw power met Duryodhana's cunning strategy. In a display of sheer might, Bhima emerged victorious, humbling the pride of the Kauravas.

But the challenges did not end there. The Kauravas, unwilling to accept defeat, proposed a final trial — a game of dice. Little did the Pandavas know that this seemingly innocent game would lead to their greatest trial yet. Shakuni, the master manipulator and uncle of the Kauravas, rigged the game in their favor, leading to the Pandavas losing everything — their kingdom, their wealth, and even their honor. Forced into exile for thirteen years, the Pandavas faced their most trying time yet.

Throughout these challenges, the Pandavas remained steadfast in their resolve, guided by the principles of righteousness and justice. Despite the odds stacked against them, they never wavered in their commitment to truth and virtue. And though their journey was fraught with obstacles and betrayal, it was their unwavering faith in dharma that ultimately led them to victory in the great war of Kurukshetra.

Thus, the Pandavas' response to the Kaurava challenges serves as a timeless reminder of the power of righteousness in the face of adversity and the triumph of good over evil.

☞Key Lessons

1. **The Power of Righteousness and Integrity:** Throughout their trials, the Pandavas remained steadfast in their commitment to righteousness (dharma) and integrity. Their unwavering adherence to these principles, even in the face of overwhelming adversity, ultimately led to their victory.

2. **Strength and Skill Combined with Wisdom:** The Pandavas' success was not only due to their individual strengths and skills but also because of the wisdom and guidance they received from Krishna. Arjuna's skill in archery, Bhima's strength in combat, and their collective strategic thinking were all enhanced by Krishna's wise counsel.

3. **Perseverance in the Face of Adversity:** Despite losing everything in the game of dice and being forced into exile, the Pandavas did not give up. They persevered through thirteen years of hardship, emerging stronger and more

determined to reclaim their rightful place.

4. **Unity and Teamwork:** The Pandavas' unity and ability to work together as a cohesive team were instrumental in their success. Each brother brought unique strengths and skills to the table, and they complemented each other perfectly.

5. **The Dangers of Arrogance and Deceit:** The Kauravas, particularly Duryodhana and Shakuni, relied on arrogance and deceit to try to defeat the Pandavas. Their unethical actions eventually led to their downfall, highlighting the perils of such behavior.

6. **Faith in Higher Principles:** The Pandavas' faith in dharma and their unwavering belief in justice and virtue were their guiding principles. This faith gave them strength and clarity, helping them navigate their many challenges.

7.(B)

Learning from Mistakes

Kauravas' Failure to Adapt

In the heart of ancient India, amidst the sprawling kingdom of Hastinapura, the tale of two families, the Pandavas and the Kauravas, unfolded. Bound by ties of blood, yet torn apart by jealousy and ambition, their story is immortalized in the pages of the Mahabharata.

The Kauravas, led by the ambitious and power-hungry Duryodhana, were a formidable force in the kingdom. Blessed with wealth, influence, and a powerful army, they seemed invincible. But it was their failure to adapt to changing circumstances that would ultimately lead to their downfall.

As tensions between the Pandavas and the Kauravas escalated, fueled by Duryodhana's envy of his cousins, the need for adaptability became increasingly apparent. Yet, blinded by his own arrogance and sense of entitlement, Duryodhana refused to heed the warnings of his well-wishers.

The first sign of the Kauravas' failure to adapt came during the game of dice, orchestrated by Duryodhana's cunning uncle, Shakuni. Knowing that Yudhishthira, the eldest Pandava, was an honorable man bound by his word, Shakuni manipulated the game to ensure the Kauravas' victory. Despite the warnings of his brothers and advisors, Duryodhana persisted, refusing to acknowledge the deceit at play. This refusal to adapt to the changing dynamics of the situation would prove to be a fatal mistake.

The game of dice not only led to the Pandavas losing their kingdom but also sparked a chain of events that would ultimately culminate in the great war of Kurukshetra. Throughout the conflict, Duryodhana's stubbornness and unwillingness to compromise only served to further alienate potential allies and weaken the Kaurava cause.

Even as the Pandavas sought peace and reconciliation, offering compromises and solutions to avoid bloodshed, Duryodhana remained obstinate, determined to assert his dominance at any cost. His refusal to adapt to the shifting landscape of politics and diplomacy only hastened the Kauravas' demise.

In the end, it was not the might of their army or the strength of their warriors that spelled the Kauravas' doom, but rather their failure to adapt to the changing tide of fate. As the great war of Kurukshetra raged on, the Kauravas found themselves outnumbered and outmaneuvered, their once-mighty empire crumbling beneath the weight of their own hubris.

Thus, the tale of the Kauravas serves as a cautionary reminder of the dangers of arrogance and inflexibility. In a world where change is constant and adaptability is key, their downfall stands as a testament to the timeless truth that those who refuse to adapt are destined to be left behind.

☞Key Lessons

1. **The Importance of Adaptability:** The Kauravas' downfall is a direct consequence of their inability to adapt to changing circumstances. Despite numerous warnings and opportunities to change their course of action, Duryodhana and his allies remained rigid in their approach, leading to their eventual destruction.

2. **The Perils of Arrogance:** Duryodhana's arrogance blinded him to the realities of his situation. His belief in his own invincibility and refusal to listen to wise counsel resulted in disastrous decisions.

3. **Listening to Wise Counsel:** Throughout the narrative, characters like Vidura and Bhishma offer wise advice to Duryodhana, urging him to seek reconciliation and avoid conflict. His refusal to heed their counsel exemplifies the

consequences of ignoring wisdom.

4. **The Consequences of Infidelity to Principles:** The Kauravas' actions, particularly the deceitful game of dice, demonstrate the consequences of unethical behavior. Their willingness to engage in dishonesty to achieve their goals ultimately led to their downfall.

5. **The Power of Diplomacy and Compromise:** Despite the Pandavas' repeated attempts at diplomacy and compromise, Duryodhana's obstinacy led to war. His refusal to negotiate or find peaceful solutions exacerbated the conflict.

6. **The Inevitable Fall of the Inflexible:** The ultimate downfall of the Kauravas underscores a timeless truth: those who are inflexible and refuse to adapt to changing circumstances are doomed to fail. The Kauravas' rigid adherence to their own flawed path led to their destruction.

7.(C)

Agility in Decision-Making

Krishna's Guidance in Crisis Situations

Amidst the epic tale of the Mahabharata, one figure stands out as the guiding light amidst the darkness of crisis – Lord Krishna. His wisdom, compassion, and divine intervention played a pivotal role in shaping the destiny of the Pandavas and the Kauravas alike.

As the rivalry between the two families reached its zenith, plunging the kingdom of Hastinapura into chaos, Krishna emerged as a beacon of hope in times of crisis. His divine guidance and unwavering support served as a source of strength for the Pandavas, guiding them through the trials and tribulations that lay ahead.

When the Pandavas faced exile in the forest, stripped of their kingdom and dignity by the deceitful game of dice orchestrated by the Kauravas, it was Krishna who offered them solace and counsel. His words of wisdom provided clarity amidst the turmoil, reminding them of their duty to uphold righteousness and justice, even in the face of adversity.

Throughout their exile, Krishna remained a steadfast companion to the Pandavas, offering them guidance and protection in their time of need. Whether it was advising Arjuna on the battlefield of Kurukshetra or mediating peace negotiations between the warring factions, Krishna's presence was felt in every aspect of the Pandavas' journey.

But Krishna's guidance extended beyond the battlefield and the palace halls. His teachings, immortalized in the Bhagavad Gita, offered profound insights into the nature of existence and the path to spiritual enlightenment. Through his discourse with Arjuna, Krishna imparted timeless wisdom on duty, righteousness, and the true nature of the self, illuminating the way forward in the darkest of times.

In crisis after crisis, Krishna remained a pillar of strength for the Pandavas, guiding them with his divine wisdom and unwavering devotion. Whether it was navigating the treacherous waters of politics or facing the horrors of war, Krishna's presence infused the Pandavas with courage and conviction, leading them ever closer to victory.

In the end, it was Krishna's guidance that paved the way for the triumph of righteousness over evil, ensuring that justice prevailed in the kingdom of Hastinapura. And though the echoes of his teachings may fade with time, the legacy of Lord Krishna's guidance in crisis situations will forever endure, a timeless reminder of the power of divine wisdom in the face of adversity.

☞Key Lessons

1. **The Power of Divine Guidance and Wisdom:** Krishna's guidance was pivotal for the Pandavas, especially during their exile and the war of Kurukshetra. His wisdom offered clarity in moments of confusion and turmoil.

2. **Upholding Righteousness and Duty:** Krishna consistently reminded the Pandavas of their duty (dharma) and the importance of upholding righteousness, even in the face of adversity.

3. **The Importance of Resilience and Courage:** Krishna's support instilled resilience and courage in the Pandavas. His presence and counsel helped them persevere through numerous trials.

4. **Adaptability and Strategic Thinking:** Krishna's strategic advice, particularly during the Kurukshetra war, demonstrated the importance of adaptability and strategic planning in overcoming challenges.

5. **The Role of Spiritual Enlightenment:** Through the Bhagavad Gita, Krishna imparted profound spiritual

wisdom, emphasizing the nature of existence, self-realization, and the pursuit of spiritual enlightenment.

6. **The Value of Mediation and Diplomacy:** Krishna's efforts to mediate peace between the Pandavas and Kauravas highlight the importance of diplomacy and seeking peaceful resolutions to conflicts.

7. **Inspiration and Leadership:** Krishna's leadership and inspirational presence motivated the Pandavas to strive for victory and justice.

8. Tactical Flexibility in Battle

In the epic Mahabharata, the battlefield serves as a crucible where tactical flexibility often determines the victor. The Pandavas, renowned for their adaptability and ingenuity, demonstrate a remarkable mastery of varied combat styles, exemplified by Arjuna's prowess with different weapons. His ability to seamlessly switch between weaponry depending on the battlefield scenario showcases the importance of versatility in tactical approaches.

Moreover, the Pandavas' adept use of deception highlights their creative problem-solving skills. By employing cunning strategies and disguises, they outmaneuver their adversaries and gain strategic advantages, showcasing the value of thinking beyond conventional tactics in battle.

Bhima, known for his strength and valor, exemplifies swift response to changing scenarios. His quick thinking and decisive actions in the heat of battle often turn the tide in favor of the Pandavas, underscoring the significance of agility and adaptability on the battlefield.

Through an exploration of these narratives, we can glean valuable insights into the principles of tactical flexibility and their relevance in modern-day strategic thinking.

8.(A)

Variety in Combat Styles

Arjuna's Mastery of Different Weapons

In the illustrious epic of the Mahabharata, one character stands out among the greatest warriors of all time – Arjuna, the third son of Pandu and the mightiest archer of his era. Yet, beyond his renowned skill with the bow and arrow, Arjuna's mastery extended to a myriad of weapons, each wielded with precision and finesse.

From a young age, Arjuna displayed a natural aptitude for combat, honing his skills under the tutelage of his guru, Dronacharya. Under his guidance, Arjuna not only mastered the art of archery but also became proficient in wielding a vast array of weapons, each with its own unique characteristics and challenges.

The Gandiva bow, gifted to him by Lord Agni, was Arjuna's primary weapon, imbued with divine power and unparalleled strength. With the Gandiva in hand, Arjuna could rain down a storm of arrows upon his enemies, striking fear into the hearts of even the mightiest warriors.

But Arjuna's prowess extended far beyond the bow. He was equally skilled in the use of the sword, the mace, the spear, and the axe, each weapon an extension of his formidable martial prowess. Whether it was the swift strikes of the sword or the crushing blows of the mace, Arjuna wielded each weapon with grace and precision, leaving his opponents in awe of his skill.

During the great war of Kurukshetra, Arjuna showcased his mastery of different weapons on the battlefield, weaving a tapestry of destruction with his unparalleled combat prowess. With his charioteer and divine guide, Lord Krishna, by his side, Arjuna became an unstoppable force, single-handedly turning the tide of battle in favor of the Pandavas.

But it was not just his physical prowess that made Arjuna a legendary warrior. His mastery of different weapons was matched only by his unwavering dedication to dharma, the righteous path. Even in the heat of battle, Arjuna adhered to the principles of honor and integrity, refusing to compromise his morals for the sake of victory.

In the end, it was Arjuna's mastery of different weapons, combined with his unshakable commitment to righteousness, that secured his place in the chronicles of history as one of the greatest warriors of all time. And though the echoes of his exploits may fade with time, the legend of Arjuna, the master of weapons, will forever endure as a testament to the power of skill, courage, and unwavering determination.

☞Key Lessons

1. **Pursuit of Excellence:** From a young age, Arjuna's dedication to mastering different weapons exemplified his relentless pursuit of excellence. His commitment to becoming the best warrior drove him to train rigorously under the guidance of his guru, Dronacharya.

2. **Versatility and Adaptability:** Arjuna's proficiency with multiple weapons, including the Gandiva bow, sword, mace, spear, and axe, showcased his versatility and adaptability on the battlefield.

3. **Harnessing Divine Strength:** The Gandiva bow, a gift from Lord Agni, symbolized the divine support and strength that Arjuna wielded in battle. His ability to harness this power made him an extraordinary warrior.

4. **Strategic Use of Skills:** Arjuna's strategic use of different weapons during the Kurukshetra war demonstrated his tactical acumen. He knew when and how to deploy his skills to maximize their impact.

5. **Commitment to Righteousness (Dharma):** Despite his formidable prowess, Arjuna's unwavering commitment to

dharma set him apart. He adhered to the principles of honor and integrity, even in the chaos of battle.

6. **Leadership and Teamwork:** With Krishna as his charioteer and guide, Arjuna demonstrated the importance of collaboration and leadership. Their partnership was pivotal in turning the tide of battle.

7. **Courage and Determination:** Arjuna's courage and determination on the battlefield exemplified his warrior spirit. His fearless approach to combat and unwavering focus were key to his victories.

8.(B)

Creative Problem-Solving

Pandavas' Use of Deception

In the grand tapestry of the Mahabharata, amidst the clash of mighty armies and the struggle for power, the Pandavas, bound by their sense of righteousness, occasionally resorted to the subtle art of deception to achieve their noble ends.

One such instance occurred during their years of exile in the forest. Duryodhana, driven by envy and malice, sought to hunt down the Pandavas and eliminate them once and for all. Aware of the dangers that lurked in the shadows, the Pandavas devised a cunning plan to outwit their adversaries.

Disguising themselves as Brahmins, the Pandavas sought refuge in the kingdom of Virata, under the guise of humble servants.

Yudhishthira assumed the role of a skilled dice player, Bhima became a cook, Arjuna a eunuch, Nakula a stable hand, and Sahadeva a cowherd. In their new identities, they lived among the common folk, biding their time until the opportune moment presented itself.

Their deception, however, did not go unnoticed. Duryodhana's spies soon discovered the whereabouts of the Pandavas and launched an attack on Virata's kingdom. Sensing the imminent danger, the Pandavas unleashed their hidden talents, revealing their true identities and rallying the people of Virata to defend their kingdom.

Arjuna, disguised as Brihannala, the eunuch, emerged as the hero of the battle, wielding his celestial bow Gandiva with unparalleled skill. Bhima, the mighty cook, unleashed his brute strength upon the enemy forces, crushing them with his bare hands. Yudhishthira, Nakula, and Sahadeva, each in their own way, fought valiantly, inspiring courage in their allies and striking fear into the hearts of their foes.

In the end, it was the Pandavas' use of deception that turned the tide of battle in their favor, thwarting Duryodhana's nefarious plans and securing victory for the kingdom of Virata. Though they had strayed from the path of truth, their actions were driven by necessity and fueled by their unwavering commitment to justice.

And so, the tale of the Pandavas' use of deception serves as a reminder that even the noblest of warriors may resort to cunning and guile in the face of overwhelming odds. For in the game of power and politics, sometimes the greatest victories are won not with swords and spears, but with the subtle art of deception.

☞ Key Lessons

1. **Adaptability in Adversity:** The Pandavas' ability to adapt to their circumstances by disguising themselves as Brahmins in the kingdom of Virata underscores their resilience and resourcefulness.

2. **Strategic Thinking:** Disguising themselves in various roles within Virata's kingdom was a strategic move that allowed the Pandavas to bide their time and prepare for future confrontations.

3. **Leveraging Hidden Talents:** While in disguise, each Pandava utilized a specific skill that contributed to their survival and eventual success. Arjuna's role as Brihannala, the eunuch, and his subsequent emergence as a hero in battle exemplify the power of leveraging hidden talents.

4. **The Ethical Boundaries of Deception:** The Pandavas' deception, though driven by necessity, raises questions about the ethical boundaries of such actions. Their ultimate goal was to uphold righteousness and justice, even if their means involved cunning.

5. **Unity and Collaboration:** The Pandavas' success relied heavily on their unity and collaboration. Each brother

played a vital role in their collective strategy, demonstrating the strength of teamwork.

6. **Courage and Bravery:** When their deception was uncovered, the Pandavas did not hesitate to reveal their true identities and defend the kingdom of Virata. Their bravery and combat skills turned the tide of battle.

7. **The Power of Intelligence Over Brute Force:** The Pandavas' use of intelligence and cunning, rather than relying solely on brute force, highlights the importance of mental acuity in overcoming adversaries.

8.(C)

Swift Response to Changing Scenarios

Bhima's Quick Thinking

One evening, as the Pandavas rested in their secluded forest camp, a sudden and unsettling sound pierced the tranquil air. Scouts reported that the fearsome demon Bakasura, notorious for his monstrous appetite and cruelty, had descended upon a nearby village. The villagers, desperate and terrified, sought refuge and aid from the Pandavas.

Yudhishthira, the eldest Pandava and their leader, called his brothers together to discuss the plight of the villagers. Although they were in exile and facing their own trials, Yudhishthira's commitment to righteousness meant they could not ignore the suffering of innocents.

Understanding the urgency, Bhima stepped forward. "Brother, let me go. I will face Bakasura and put an end to his terror. The people should not suffer while we have the strength to help."

Yudhishthira agreed, knowing well Bhima's unparalleled strength. However, he cautioned, "Bhima, Bakasura is cunning and powerful. You must be vigilant and use not just your strength, but your mind as well."

With these words, Bhima set out towards the village. As he walked, he pondered his strategy. Physical strength alone, he knew, might not be enough against such a formidable foe. He needed a plan.

Upon reaching the village, Bhima saw the terror in the eyes of the villagers. He reassured them, "Fear not, for I will protect you. Stay inside your homes and do not come out until it is safe."

As night fell, Bhima ventured into the dark forest where Bakasura was last seen. He carried with him a massive pot of food, knowing that the demon's hunger often drove his actions. Soon enough, Bakasura emerged from the shadows, his eyes gleaming with malevolent intent.

"What is this?" Bakasura roared, seeing the food. "A meal brought to me willingly?"

Bhima, calm and composed, replied, "Yes, mighty Bakasura. I have brought you a feast. Eat to your heart's content."

As Bakasura began to devour the food, Bhima's plan took shape. He had laced the food with a potent, albeit non-lethal, sedative made from forest herbs. As Bakasura ate greedily, he began to feel drowsy, his monstrous strength ebbing.

Seeing the demon's reaction, Bhima wasted no time. He approached Bakasura, who, now sluggish and weakened, attempted to rise but stumbled. "You dared to poison me?" Bakasura snarled weakly.

"No," Bhima replied calmly, "I simply evened the odds."

With a swift and powerful motion, Bhima grappled with the demon, using his immense strength to subdue Bakasura. The fight was fierce, but with Bakasura weakened by the sedative, Bhima's victory was assured. After a prolonged struggle, he managed to break the demon's spine, ending his reign of terror once and for all.

With Bakasura defeated, Bhima returned to the village, carrying the demon's lifeless body. The villagers emerged, their fear turning to awe and gratitude. "You have saved us, great Bhima!" they cried. "We are forever in your debt."

Bhima smiled and replied, "It is our duty to protect the innocent. Live in peace, for the threat is no more."

When he returned to his brothers, Bhima recounted the tale. Yudhishthira praised him, saying, "Bhima, today you have shown that true strength lies not only in might but in wisdom and quick thinking."

☙❧☙❧☙❧☙❧☙❧☙❧❧

☞Key Lessons

1. **Strength Alone is Not Enough:** While Bhima was renowned for his immense physical strength, the situation with Bakasura required more than brute force. Bhima understood that defeating the demon would necessitate strategic thinking and clever planning. This teaches us that relying solely on one's strengths is not always sufficient; it is important to combine physical prowess with intelligence and strategy.

2. **Adaptability and Flexibility:** Bhima's approach to the crisis demonstrated his ability to adapt and be flexible. Instead of charging at Bakasura head-on, he devised a plan that suited the circumstances. Being adaptable and flexible in the face of challenges often leads to better outcomes than rigidly sticking to a single method.

3. **Using Resources Wisely:** Bhima used the resources available to him—the knowledge of forest herbs and the sedative properties they possessed—to his advantage. This highlights the importance of utilizing available resources creatively and efficiently to solve problems.

4. **Thinking Ahead:** Bhima anticipated Bakasura's behavior and planned accordingly by lacing the food with a

sedative. This foresight helped him neutralize the demon's threat effectively. Thinking ahead and anticipating possible scenarios can help in making better decisions and achieving desired results.

5. **Protecting the Innocent:** Bhima's primary motivation was to protect the innocent villagers. This underscores the value of altruism and the importance of using one's abilities to help others. It reminds us that true heroism lies in safeguarding and serving those who are vulnerable.

6. **Leadership and Responsibility:** When Bhima took on the responsibility of facing Bakasura, he demonstrated true leadership. Leaders must sometimes make difficult decisions and take on dangerous tasks to protect their people. Responsibility and courage are essential traits of effective leadership.

7. **Wisdom in Action:** Yudhishthira's advice to Bhima to use his mind as well as his strength emphasizes the importance of wisdom. Bhima's actions were guided by wisdom, not just impulsive bravery. Applying wisdom in action leads to more sustainable and effective solutions.

8. **Humility in Victory:** After defeating Bakasura, Bhima did not boast about his victory. Instead, he reassured the villagers and humbly accepted their gratitude, emphasizing duty over glory. Humility in victory is a noble trait that garners respect and trust.

9. **Teamwork and Trust:** The story also reflects the trust and teamwork among the Pandavas. Yudhishthira trusted Bhima's abilities, and Bhima sought his brother's counsel. Successful outcomes often depend on mutual trust and collaboration within a team.

10. **Moral Integrity:** Even in a situation where deception was used, Bhima maintained moral integrity by ensuring the sedative was non-lethal. This teaches that ethical considerations should not be abandoned even in desperate situations.

9. Operational Momentum and Sustaining Progress

In the grand narrative of the Mahabharata, the concept of operational momentum emerges as a critical factor in determining the course of battles and campaigns. Characters like Abhimanyu, known for his valor and unwavering determination, epitomize the idea of unstoppable momentum on the battlefield. His relentless charge into enemy lines during the Chakravyuha formation stands as a testament to the power of sustained momentum in achieving strategic objectives.

Similarly, figures like Bheeshma exemplify the importance of endurance and persistence in sustaining progress over the long term. Despite facing numerous challenges and setbacks, Bheeshma's resolve remains unshaken, showcasing the role of steadfastness in overcoming obstacles and maintaining operational momentum.

Karna, renowned for his unyielding spirit and loyalty, further illustrates the concept of sustaining progress in the face of adversity. His unwavering commitment to his principles and cause serves as an example of how resilience and steadfastness can help navigate through challenging circumstances and maintain operational momentum.

By examining these characters and their stories, we can gain valuable insights into the dynamics of operational momentum and the strategies for sustaining progress in the midst of challenges and uncertainties.

9.(A)

Momentum in Battle

Abhimanyu's Unstoppable Charge

In the vast expanse of the Mahabharata, amidst the tumultuous battlefield of Kurukshetra, one warrior shone with an unstoppable fervor – Abhimanyu, the valiant son of Arjuna and Subhadra. His tale is etched in the history as a testament to bravery, courage, and the indomitable spirit of youth.

As the war raged on, the Kaurava forces, led by their most formidable warriors, sought to break the resolve of the Pandavas and their allies. In response, Arjuna, the mightiest of warriors, entrusted his young son Abhimanyu with a task of great peril – penetrating the Chakravyuha, a formidable formation devised by the Kauravas.

Though barely a teenager, Abhimanyu possessed the skill and valor of a seasoned warrior. With his father's blessings and the divine guidance of Lord Krishna, he embarked on his daring mission, his heart ablaze with determination and courage.

As the Pandava forces engaged the Kauravas in battle, Abhimanyu charged forth, his chariot cutting through the enemy ranks like a thunderbolt. With his swift movements and unmatched skill, he cleaved through the opposing forces, leaving a trail of devastation in his wake.

But the true test awaited him at the heart of the Chakravyuha, a labyrinthine formation designed to ensnare and overwhelm the unwary. Undeterred by the daunting challenge that lay ahead, Abhimanyu plunged headlong into the fray, his courage undiminished by the odds stacked against him.

With a single-minded focus and unwavering determination, Abhimanyu fought his way through the maze of enemy warriors, his blade flashing in the sunlight as he struck down all who stood in his path. Despite the ferocity of the Kaurava onslaught, he remained undaunted, his resolve unshakable in the face of adversity.

But alas, fate had other plans for the young warrior. Trapped within the Chakravyuha with no means of escape, Abhimanyu found himself surrounded by the enemy forces, his valor alone insufficient to overcome the overwhelming odds. Though he fought with the strength of ten men, he was ultimately overwhelmed by the sheer numbers arrayed against him.

Yet even in death, Abhimanyu's legacy lived on, a shining example of courage and heroism for generations to come. His unstoppable charge through the ranks of the enemy forces served as a testament to the indomitable spirit of youth and the power of valor in the face of adversity.

And though his life was cut short on that fateful day, Abhimanyu's name would forever be remembered as a symbol of bravery and sacrifice, immortalized in the pages of the Mahabharata as one of its greatest heroes.

☞Key Lessons

1. **Courage in the Face of Adversity:** Abhimanyu's willingness to enter the Chakravyuha, knowing the dangers that lay within, exemplifies immense courage. This teaches us that true bravery involves facing challenges head-on, even when the odds are overwhelmingly against us.

2. **Determination and Perseverance:** Despite being only a teenager, Abhimanyu showed unwavering determination and perseverance. His relentless spirit serves as a reminder that age is not a barrier to achieving greatness. Determination can drive individuals to accomplish remarkable feats, irrespective of their experience or age.

3. **Skill and Preparation:** Abhimanyu's prowess on the battlefield was a result of rigorous training and preparation. This highlights the importance of developing

one's skills and being prepared for any challenge that may come. Excellence is often the product of consistent practice and dedication.

4. **Leadership and Responsibility:** Entrusted with a crucial task by his father, Abhimanyu accepted the responsibility without hesitation. His actions demonstrate the importance of stepping up and taking charge, especially in critical situations. Leadership often involves taking on difficult and dangerous tasks for the greater good.

5. **Sacrifice for a Noble Cause:** Abhimanyu's willingness to lay down his life for the Pandavas' cause underscores the value of sacrifice. Sometimes, achieving a greater good requires personal sacrifices. This lesson is about selflessness and the willingness to endure personal loss for the benefit of others.

6. **The Indomitable Spirit of Youth:** Abhimanyu's story is a celebration of youthful vigor and potential. It teaches that youth, when guided by purpose and valor, can achieve extraordinary things. The spirit of youth should be harnessed for noble and righteous causes.

7. **Legacy and Heroism:** Although Abhimanyu's life was tragically cut short, his heroism left a lasting legacy. This teaches us that the impact of our actions can transcend our lifetime. Acts of bravery and selflessness can inspire future generations and leave an indelible mark on history.

8. **The Role of Fate and Destiny:** Abhimanyu's fate in the Chakravyuha also reflects on the role of destiny in life. Despite one's best efforts and intentions, outcomes are sometimes beyond control. This lesson reminds us to accept the role of fate with grace, acknowledging that not all battles can be won.

9. **Importance of Knowledge:** Abhimanyu knew how to enter the Chakravyuha but did not know how to exit it, due to his incomplete training. This highlights the importance of comprehensive knowledge and continuous learning. It is essential to understand all aspects of a challenge before undertaking it.

10. **Unity and Support:** Abhimanyu's story also indirectly stresses the need for unity and support. His tragic end could have been different if the other Pandavas had been able to support him in breaking out of the formation. This underscores the value of teamwork and collective effort in overcoming significant challenges.

9.(B)

Endurance and Persistence

Bheeshma's Resolve

In the vast expanse of the Mahabharata, amidst the clash of empires and the struggles of kings, one figure stands out as a beacon of unwavering resolve – Bheeshma, the grand patriarch of the Kuru dynasty. His tale is one of duty, honor, and the sacrifices made in service of righteousness.

Born of the union between King Shantanu and the river goddess Ganga, Bheeshma was destined for greatness from the moment of his birth. Gifted with immortality and unmatched prowess in battle, he became the cornerstone of the Kuru dynasty, revered by both friend and foe alike.

But it was not his strength alone that earned Bheeshma his legendary status. It was his unyielding resolve to uphold dharma, the righteous path, even in the face of seemingly insurmountable odds. Throughout his long and illustrious life, Bheeshma remained steadfast in his commitment to his principles, never wavering in the face of temptation or adversity.

His resolve was tested time and again, most notably during the infamous game of dice that led to the exile of the Pandavas and the eventual outbreak of war. Despite his deep love for his nephews, the Pandavas, Bheeshma remained bound by his oath of loyalty to the Kuru dynasty, forced to watch in silence as injustice unfolded before his eyes.

Yet even as he fought on the side of the Kauravas in the great war of Kurukshetra, Bheeshma's resolve never faltered. Though he knew that the cause for which he fought was unjust, he remained true to his duty as a warrior and a protector of his kingdom, refusing to abandon his post until the bitter end.

In the final days of the war, as the battlefield lay littered with the bodies of the fallen, Bheeshma lay mortally wounded, pierced by a thousand arrows yet still clinging to life. It was then that he uttered his famous vow – to lay down his arms and await death on a bed of arrows until the time came for him to depart from this world.

And so, surrounded by his loved ones and his enemies alike, Bheeshma breathed his last, his resolve unbroken even in death. Though he may have been laid low by the passage of time, his legacy lived on, a testament to the power of unwavering resolve in the face of adversity, immortalized in the pages of the Mahabharata for all time.

☞Key Lessons

1. **Unwavering Commitment to Duty:** Bheeshma's life is a profound example of steadfast adherence to duty (dharma). He remained loyal to his commitments, even when they led him into difficult and morally complex situations. This teaches the importance of honoring one's promises and responsibilities, regardless of personal cost.

2. **Sacrifice for a Greater Cause:** Bheeshma's vow of celibacy, taken to ensure his father's happiness and the stability of the Kuru dynasty, exemplifies the spirit of self-sacrifice. He placed the welfare of others above his desires, showing that true leadership often involves making personal sacrifices for the greater good.

3. **Adherence to Principles:** Throughout his life, Bheeshma adhered strictly to his principles, demonstrating the value of integrity. Even when faced with the prospect of fighting against his beloved Pandavas, he did not waver from his duty as the guardian of the Kuru throne. This underscores the importance of maintaining one's principles, even in the face of immense pressure.

4. **Resilience in Adversity:** Bheeshma's ability to remain resolute, even when mortally wounded and lying on a bed of arrows, illustrates incredible resilience. His determination to fulfill his duties until the very end is a

powerful lesson in perseverance and resilience in the face of suffering.

5. **Complexity of Morality:** Bheeshma's story highlights the complexity of moral decisions. He found himself in situations where his duties conflicted with his personal values, particularly during the Kurukshetra war. This teaches that life often presents complex moral dilemmas, and navigating them requires deep contemplation and courage.

6. **Respect for Opponents:** Despite fighting for the Kauravas, Bheeshma maintained a profound respect for the Pandavas and their righteousness. This teaches the importance of respecting one's opponents and acknowledging their virtues, even in conflict.

7. **Wisdom and Guidance:** Bheeshma was a source of wisdom and guidance for both the Kauravas and the Pandavas. His ability to offer counsel and share his knowledge, even with those on the opposing side, demonstrates the value of wisdom and the importance of imparting knowledge selflessly.

8. **Legacy of Righteousness:** Bheeshma's life left an enduring legacy of righteousness and duty. His actions and choices became a guiding example for future generations. This teaches that living a life of principle and integrity can leave a lasting impact beyond one's lifetime.

9. **Acceptance of Fate:** Bheeshma's acceptance of his fate, particularly his vow to await death on the bed of arrows until the right time, shows a profound acceptance of destiny. This teaches the importance of embracing one's fate with grace and dignity.

10. **Balance of Strength and Compassion:** While Bheeshma was a formidable warrior, he was also compassionate and wise. This balance between strength and compassion is essential for true leadership and effective decision-making.

9.(C)

Steadfastness in Adversity

Karna's Unyielding Spirit

In the grand tapestry of the Mahabharata, amidst the clash of kingdoms and the struggle for supremacy, one figure stands out as a beacon of unwavering spirit – Karna, the noble son of Surya, the sun god, and Kunti, the mother of the Pandavas. His tale is one of resilience, honor, and the enduring quest for acceptance.

Born to Kunti before her marriage to Pandu, Karna's life was marked by adversity from the very beginning. Rejected by his mother and raised as a charioteer's son, he faced ridicule and discrimination at every turn. Yet, despite the hardships he endured, Karna's spirit remained unbroken, his resolve unyielding in the face of adversity.

From a young age, Karna displayed exceptional skill and valor, earning the admiration of all who crossed his path. Blessed with the divine armor and earrings bestowed upon him by his father, Surya, he became an unparalleled warrior, feared by his enemies and revered by his allies.

But it was not just his prowess in battle that set Karna apart — it was his unwavering sense of honor and integrity. Despite his illegitimate birth and the scorn he faced from society, Karna remained steadfast in his principles, refusing to compromise his morals for the sake of acceptance.

Throughout his life, Karna faced numerous challenges, each more daunting than the last. From the moment he learned of his true parentage to his fateful encounter with Lord Krishna on the battlefield of Kurukshetra, his journey was marked by hardship and sacrifice.

Yet, through it all, Karna's spirit remained unbroken. Even when faced with the ultimate betrayal at the hands of his closest friend, Duryodhana, who revealed his true lineage to the world in a moment of desperation, Karna did not waver. Instead, he faced his destiny with courage and dignity, embracing his role as a warrior and a hero till the very end.

In the final moments of his life, as he lay mortally wounded on the battlefield, Karna's spirit soared high, his soul untainted by regret or bitterness. Though he may have been denied the acceptance and recognition he so desperately sought in life, in death, he found redemption, his unwavering spirit shining bright for all to see.

And so, as the flames of his funeral pyre consumed his mortal remains, Karna's legacy lived on, a testament to the power of resilience, honor, and the unyielding spirit of a true warrior, immortalized in the pages of the Mahabharata for all time.

☞Key Lessons

1. **Resilience in Adversity:** Karna's life was filled with hardships from the beginning. Despite being born to a royal mother, he was abandoned and raised by a charioteer. He faced discrimination and ridicule throughout his life, yet he remained resilient. This teaches us the importance of perseverance and strength in the face of adversity.

2. **Self-Belief and Determination:** Despite the societal scorn and his illegitimate birth, Karna believed in his abilities and strived to become a great warrior. His self-belief and determination led him to achieve unparalleled skill in archery and combat. This underscores the power of self-belief and determination in achieving one's goals.

3. **Honor and Integrity:** Karna's unwavering sense of honor and integrity set him apart. Even when faced with difficult choices, he adhered to his principles and refused to compromise his morals. This highlights the importance of maintaining one's honor and integrity, regardless of external pressures.

4. **Loyalty and Friendship:** Karna remained loyal to Duryodhana, who was the first to recognize and support him despite his lowly birth. This loyalty, although it eventually led to his downfall, demonstrates the value of standing by those who have stood by you, showcasing the strength of true friendship and loyalty.

5. **Courage in the Face of Fate:** Throughout his life, Karna faced numerous revelations and challenges, including learning about his true parentage and dealing with societal rejection. He faced these challenges with courage and accepted his fate with dignity, teaching us to confront life's difficulties with bravery.

6. **Sacrifice and Selflessness:** Karna made significant sacrifices throughout his life, including giving away his divine armor and earrings, which made him vulnerable in battle. His selflessness and willingness to give up even his greatest assets for others highlight the virtue of sacrifice.

7. **The Complexity of Morality:** Karna's story illustrates the complexity of moral decisions. Despite being on the side perceived as unjust (the Kauravas), his personal qualities of honor, loyalty, and bravery were admirable. This teaches that morality is often complex and multi-faceted, and individuals can possess both virtues and flaws.

8. **Seeking Acceptance and Recognition:** Karna's quest for acceptance and recognition, despite his extraordinary talents and virtues, shows the deep human need for

validation. It reminds us of the importance of acknowledging and valuing people's worth and contributions, regardless of their background.

9. **Facing Betrayal with Dignity:** Even when he was betrayed and his true lineage was revealed, Karna faced the situation with dignity and courage. This teaches the importance of handling betrayal and difficult truths with grace and composure.

10. **Redemption and Legacy:** Karna's unwavering spirit and his heroic actions on the battlefield earned him redemption. His legacy, immortalized in the Mahabharata, is a testament to the enduring power of resilience, honor, and courage. This shows that one's actions and spirit can leave a lasting legacy, regardless of life's injustices.

10. Environmental Analysis and Adaptation

In the epic saga of the Mahabharata, the ability to analyze and adapt to the environment plays a crucial role in the outcomes of various events. Characters are often faced with diverse landscapes, climates, and political situations, requiring them to assess their surroundings and adjust their strategies accordingly.

One such example is the Kurukshetra battlefield, known for its diverse terrain and strategic challenges. Understanding the nuances of the battlefield, including its geography, vegetation, and natural features, is crucial for devising effective battle plans. Characters like Bhishma and Drona demonstrate the importance of environmental analysis in their strategic positioning and maneuvering during the war.

The Pandavas' exile in the forest also highlights the significance of adapting to different climates and environments. Through their resilience and resourcefulness, they not only survived but also thrived in the harsh wilderness, showcasing the importance of environmental adaptation in challenging circumstances.

Additionally, Krishna's diplomacy exemplifies the need to navigate complex political landscapes. His ability to understand the motives and intentions of various factions and to forge alliances based on this understanding demonstrates the importance of environmental analysis in political decision-making.

By exploring these aspects of environmental analysis and adaptation in the Mahabharata, we can glean valuable insights into the importance of understanding and adapting to diverse environments in both strategic and personal contexts.

10.(A)

Understanding Terrain

Lessons from the Kurukshetra Landscape

In the ancient land of Kurukshetra, where the great war of the Mahabharata unfolded, every blade of grass, every pebble, and every tree bore witness to the tumultuous events that shaped the destiny of kingdoms and the lives of heroes. Amidst the chaos of battle and the clash of mighty armies, the landscape of Kurukshetra became a silent yet profound teacher, imparting timeless lessons that transcended the boundaries of time and space.

As the sun rose over the blood-stained battlefield, casting its golden light upon the fallen warriors and the grieving families left behind, the landscape of Kurukshetra spoke of the impermanence of life and the inevitability of change. In the ebb and flow of the river of time, it reminded all who beheld its vast expanse that nothing in this world is permanent, and that even the mightiest empires must one day crumble to dust.

Amidst the charred remains of broken chariots and shattered weapons, the landscape of Kurukshetra whispered of the futility of violence and the tragic cost of war. It bore witness to the countless lives lost in the pursuit of power and glory, reminding humanity of the senselessness of conflict and the need for compassion and understanding.

But amidst the devastation and despair, the landscape of Kurukshetra also offered a glimmer of hope – a reminder of the resilience of the human spirit and the power of redemption. For even in the darkest of times, amidst the chaos and confusion of battle, acts of bravery and selflessness shone like beacons of light, illuminating the path to a brighter future.

And so, as the echoes of battle faded into the distance and the winds of change swept across the plains of Kurukshetra, the lessons of the battlefield remained etched in the hearts and minds of all who had borne witness to its trials and tribulations. For in the crucible of war, amidst the clash of steel and the roar of thunder, the landscape of Kurukshetra had become not just a battleground, but a sacred teacher, imparting lessons of wisdom and truth that would echo through the ages for generations to come.

☞ Key Lessons

1. **Impermanence of Life:** The landscape of Kurukshetra reflects the impermanent nature of life. It reminds us that everything in this world, including great empires and powerful individuals, is subject to change and eventual decline. This teaches us the importance of appreciating the present moment and not becoming attached to worldly possessions or power.

2. **Futility of Violence:** The devastation left behind by the war highlights the futility of violence and the tragic consequences of conflict. It serves as a stark reminder that war only brings suffering and loss, emphasizing the need for peaceful resolution of conflicts and the importance of compassion and understanding.

3. **Resilience of the Human Spirit:** Despite the horrors of war, the landscape of Kurukshetra also offers a message of hope. It showcases the resilience of the human spirit and the capacity for individuals to rise above adversity. This teaches us that even in the darkest of times, acts of bravery, selflessness, and compassion can lead to a brighter future.

4. **Power of Redemption:** The battlefield of Kurukshetra is not just a place of death and destruction but also of redemption. It highlights the possibility of personal

transformation and the power of individuals to overcome their past mistakes. This teaches us that no matter how dire the circumstances, there is always a chance for redemption and renewal.

5. **Importance of Wisdom and Truth:** The landscape of Kurukshetra is depicted as a teacher, imparting lessons of wisdom and truth. It underscores the importance of seeking knowledge, understanding, and discernment in order to navigate the complexities of life. This teaches us to value wisdom and truth as guiding principles in our own lives.

6. **Echoes Through Generations:** The lessons of Kurukshetra are said to echo through the ages, reminding us of the enduring relevance of these teachings. They serve as a timeless guide for future generations, offering insights into human nature, morality, and the pursuit of a meaningful life.

10.(B)

Adapting to Climate

Pandavas' Survival in the Forest

Once upon a time, in the ancient land of Bharat, there lived five brothers known as the Pandavas. Yudhishthira, Bhima, Arjuna, Nakula, and Sahadeva were the sons of King Pandu, but they were raised by their mother Kunti in the forest, far away from the royal palace.

The Pandavas' exile began after their cousin Duryodhana, fueled by jealousy and ambition, conspired against them and tricked them into a game of dice. Yudhishthira, the eldest brother, lost everything in the game – his kingdom, his wealth, and even his own freedom. As per the rules of the game, the Pandavas were to spend twelve years in exile followed by one year in anonymity.

With heavy hearts but unwavering resolve, the Pandavas set out for the forests. Their journey was fraught with challenges, but they faced them with courage and wisdom.

As they ventured deeper into the wilderness, they encountered sages and learned from them the art of survival in the forest. They learned to identify edible roots and berries, to hunt for game, and to build shelter from natural resources. Despite the hardships, the Pandavas remained united and resolute in their determination to uphold righteousness.

One day, while wandering through the dense forest, the Pandavas stumbled upon a beautiful clearing with a tranquil lake. They decided to rest there for a while, seeking solace amidst the serenity of nature. Little did they know that their peaceful respite would soon be disrupted.

As they were resting, a monstrous demon named Hidimba emerged from the shadows, hungry for flesh and blood. With his terrifying appearance and ferocious demeanor, he charged towards the Pandavas, intent on devouring them.

Quick to react, Bhima, the strongest of the brothers, stepped forward to confront the demon. A fierce battle ensued between Bhima and Hidimba, each displaying unmatched strength and valor. Despite Hidimba's formidable powers, Bhima fought with unwavering determination, fueled by his love and duty towards his brothers.

In the end, it was Bhima who emerged victorious, vanquishing the demon and saving his brothers from certain doom.

Impressed by Bhima's bravery and prowess, Hidimba's sister, Hidimbi, approached the Pandavas and expressed her gratitude.

Hidimbi, a beautiful and kind-hearted woman, offered her assistance to the Pandavas during their exile. Touched by her sincerity, the Pandavas accepted her offer, and Hidimbi became a trusted ally and friend.

Together, the Pandavas and Hidimbi continued their journey through the forest, facing numerous trials and tribulations along the way. But through their unwavering faith in each other and their commitment to righteousness, they persevered, emerging stronger and more resilient than ever before.

And thus, amidst the challenges of the wilderness, the Pandavas forged bonds of friendship and loyalty that would guide them through the darkest of times, leading them ever closer to their ultimate destiny.

☞ Key Lessons

1. **Resilience in Adversity:** Despite losing everything in a deceitful game of dice, the Pandavas did not lose hope or succumb to despair. Instead, they embraced their exile with courage and determination, showing resilience in the face of adversity.

    This teaches us the importance of resilience in overcoming challenges. Life may present us with difficult circumstances, but it is our resilience that allows us to persevere and emerge stronger.

2. **Unity and Brotherhood:** Throughout their exile, the Pandavas remained united as brothers, supporting each other through thick and thin. Their unity was their strength, helping them navigate the challenges of the forest.

    This highlights the importance of unity and cooperation, showing that together, we can overcome even the toughest of challenges.

3. **Resourcefulness and Adaptability:** In the forest, the Pandavas learned to be resourceful, utilizing the natural resources around them for survival. They learned to identify edible plants, hunt for food, and build shelter.

    This teaches us the importance of adaptability and resourcefulness. Life often presents us with unforeseen circumstances, and being adaptable and resourceful allows us to find solutions even in challenging situations.

4. **Courage and Bravery:** When faced with the monstrous demon Hidimba, it was Bhima's courage and bravery that saved the day. He fearlessly confronted the demon, putting his own life at risk to protect his brothers.

    This illustrates the importance of courage in the face of danger. Sometimes, we must confront our fears head-on to overcome obstacles and protect those we care about.

5. **Friendship and Kindness:** Hidimbi's act of kindness towards the Pandavas, despite her brother's defeat, highlights the power of friendship and compassion. Her friendship with the Pandavas became a source of support and assistance during their exile.

   This shows us the impact of kindness and friendship in our lives. Being kind and compassionate towards others can lead to unexpected friendships and support when we need it most.

6. **Faith in Righteousness:** Throughout their journey, the Pandavas remained committed to upholding righteousness and dharma. This unwavering faith in doing what is right guided their actions and decisions.

   This teaches us the importance of staying true to our principles and values, even in difficult times. Upholding righteousness can lead us on the path to self-discovery and fulfillment.

10.(C)

Navigating Political Landscapes:

Krishna's Diplomacy

In the ancient land of Bharat, where righteousness and treachery clashed in the epic tale of the Mahabharata, there existed a figure whose wisdom and diplomacy shaped the destiny of nations. This figure was none other than Lord Krishna, the divine incarnation of Vishnu.

As the great war between the Pandavas and the Kauravas loomed on the horizon, Krishna understood that victory could not be achieved through strength alone. It would require strategy, cunning, and diplomacy. With this knowledge, Krishna embarked on a mission to secure allies for the Pandavas and weaken the forces of their adversaries.

Krishna's first diplomatic endeavor took him to the kingdom of the Yadavas, his own clan. He knew that their support would be crucial in the upcoming conflict. With his charismatic charm and persuasive words, Krishna convinced the Yadava king, Ugrasena, and his subjects to pledge their allegiance to the Pandavas. Thus, the mighty Yadava army joined the ranks of the Pandava alliance.

But Krishna's diplomatic efforts did not stop there. He understood the importance of building alliances with neighboring kingdoms to bolster the Pandavas' strength. With strategic precision, Krishna approached rulers across the land, offering them incentives and assurances of prosperity in exchange for their support.

One such ruler was the powerful king of the Matsya kingdom, Virata. Recognizing the value of Krishna's alliance, Virata agreed to provide his army and resources to aid the Pandavas in their cause. With the addition of the Matsya forces, the Pandava alliance grew even stronger, striking fear into the hearts of their enemies.

Yet, Krishna's diplomacy extended beyond the realm of military alliances. He also sought to sow discord among the ranks of the Kauravas, weakening their resolve from within. Through subtle manipulation and clever schemes, Krishna planted seeds of doubt and mistrust among the Kaurava princes, sowing the seeds of their eventual downfall.

One of Krishna's most famous diplomatic maneuvers occurred during the peace negotiations before the war. As the envoy of the Pandavas, Krishna approached the Kaurava court with a proposal for a peaceful resolution to the conflict. With his silver tongue and persuasive arguments, Krishna laid out terms that favored the Pandavas while appearing fair and just to the Kauravas.

However, despite Krishna's best efforts, the Kauravas refused to concede, blinded by their pride and ambition. And so, the stage was set for the great war of Kurukshetra, where Krishna would serve not only as a diplomat but also as a charioteer, advisor, and divine protector of the righteous.

In the end, it was Krishna's diplomacy that tipped the scales of fate in favor of the Pandavas. Through his cunning strategies and unwavering devotion to righteousness, Krishna ensured that justice prevailed and dharma triumphed over adharma. And though the war brought much sorrow and devastation, it also heralded the dawn of a new era, guided by the timeless principles of truth, duty, and compassion.

☞ Key Lessons

1. **Wisdom in Strategy:** Krishna's approach to the war demonstrates the importance of strategic thinking. He understood that victory required more than just military might; it needed careful planning, alliances, and the weakening of the enemy's resolve.

2. **Effective Communication:** Krishna's ability to persuade and negotiate highlights the importance of effective

communication in diplomacy. His words were not only persuasive but also strategic, aimed at achieving specific goals.

3. **Building Alliances:** Krishna's success lay in his ability to forge alliances with other kingdoms. This underscores the importance of building strong relationships and alliances to achieve common goals.

4. **Understanding Human Psychology:** Krishna's manipulation of the Kaurava princes demonstrates an understanding of human psychology. He knew how to exploit their weaknesses and sow discord among them, weakening their unity.

5. **Balance of Power:** Krishna's diplomacy ensured a balance of power in the war. By securing alliances and weakening the Kauravas, he ensured a more balanced battlefield, increasing the Pandavas' chances of victory.

6. **Conflict Resolution:** Despite his efforts for peace, Krishna was also prepared for war. This teaches us the importance of seeking peaceful resolutions to conflicts but also being prepared to defend oneself if necessary.

7. **Upholding Dharma:** Throughout his diplomatic endeavors, Krishna remained committed to upholding dharma, the righteous path. This shows the importance of moral integrity in diplomacy, even in the midst of conflict.

11. Situational Strategies in Complex Scenarios

In the epic narrative of the Mahabharata, characters often find themselves embroiled in complex and multifaceted situations that require nuanced and adaptive strategies. Whether faced with diplomatic challenges, political intrigue, or internal conflicts, the characters demonstrate a range of situational strategies to navigate these complex scenarios.

The Pandavas' ability to form and manage alliances serves as a prime example of responding to diplomatic challenges. Throughout their journey, they forge strategic alliances with various kings and warriors, such as King Virata and the Yadavas, to bolster their forces and strengthen their position against the Kauravas.

Krishna, on the other hand, demonstrates a different kind of strategy in dealing with intrigue. His Machiavellian moves, including his manipulation of the game of dice and orchestration of events to weaken the Kauravas, highlight the importance of strategic thinking and calculated deception in navigating complex political landscapes.

Furthermore, Draupadi's role in resolving disputes within the court of Hastinapura showcases the importance of managing internal conflicts. Her wisdom and composure in the face of adversity, particularly during the dice game incident, exemplify the need for effective conflict resolution strategies in complex social settings.

11.(A)

Responding to Diplomatic Challenges

Pandavas' Alliances

In the ancient land of Bharat, where the winds of destiny blew fiercely across the battlefield of Kurukshetra, the story of the Mahabharata unfolded amidst alliances forged through blood, loyalty, and honor. At the heart of these alliances stood the Pandavas, five brothers bound by the ties of kinship and righteousness.

The journey of the Pandavas' alliances began in the aftermath of a deceitful game of dice, where they were stripped of their kingdom and exiled to the forests for twelve years, followed by a year in disguise. Determined to reclaim their rightful inheritance and uphold the principles of dharma, the Pandavas embarked on a quest to seek allies who would stand by them in their time of need.

Their first ally was none other than Lord Krishna himself, the divine incarnation of Vishnu. Krishna, recognizing the righteousness of the Pandavas' cause, pledged his unwavering support to them. With his divine guidance and strategic counsel, Krishna became the linchpin of the Pandavas' alliance, guiding them through the trials and tribulations that lay ahead.

But Krishna was not the only ally to join the Pandavas' cause. Across the vast expanse of Bharat, rulers and warriors alike were drawn to the banner of righteousness that the Pandavas upheld. One such ally was King Virata of the Matsya kingdom, who offered his army and resources to aid the Pandavas in their quest for justice.

Another crucial alliance was forged with the mighty Yadavas, Krishna's own clan. Led by the valiant warrior Satyaki, the Yadava army bolstered the Pandavas' forces, turning the tide of battle in their favor. Together, the Pandavas and the Yadavas fought side by side, their bonds of brotherhood unbreakable in the face of adversity.

But perhaps the most unexpected alliance of all was with the exiled prince of the Kauravas, Karna. Despite being born to the enemy camp, Karna's sense of honor and loyalty led him to pledge his allegiance to the Pandavas. In a display of unparalleled courage and sacrifice, Karna laid down his life on the battlefield, fighting alongside his newfound brothers until his last breath.

As the war of Kurukshetra raged on, the Pandavas' alliances were tested like never before. But through courage, sacrifice, and unwavering loyalty, they emerged victorious, their enemies vanquished, and dharma restored to its rightful place.

And though the scars of battle may have marred the landscape of Bharat, the bonds of brotherhood forged amidst the chaos would endure for generations to come, a testament to the enduring power of love, loyalty, and righteousness.

☞Key Lessons

1. **The Power of Unity:** The Pandavas' alliance with various kingdoms and warriors demonstrates the power of unity in achieving common goals. By forging strong alliances, they were able to strengthen their position and overcome formidable challenges.

2. **The Importance of Allies:** Allies play a crucial role in times of need. The Pandavas' allies, including Lord Krishna, King Virata, the Yadavas, and even Karna, provided them with support, resources, and strategic guidance that proved instrumental in their success.

3. **Loyalty and Honor:** The bonds of brotherhood between the Pandavas and their allies were built on a foundation of loyalty and honor. Despite facing difficult circumstances, they remained committed to their cause and to each other, showcasing the importance of these values in alliances.

4. **Forgiveness and Redemption:** The alliance with Karna highlights the themes of forgiveness and redemption. Despite his past actions and his allegiance to the Kauravas, Karna was given a chance for redemption through his alliance with the Pandavas, ultimately sacrificing his life for their cause.

5. **Strategic Thinking:** The Pandavas' alliances were not just based on emotion but also on strategic thinking. They carefully chose their allies based on their strengths and resources, maximizing their chances of success in the war.

6. **The Impact of Leadership:** The leadership of figures like Lord Krishna and the Pandavas was crucial in forming and maintaining alliances. Their wisdom, charisma, and strategic acumen were instrumental in rallying allies to their cause and keeping their alliance strong.

11.(B)

Dealing with Intrigue

Krishna's Machiavellian Moves

In the ancient Bharat, amidst the epic saga of the Mahabharata, there existed a figure whose cunning and strategic acumen surpassed all others. This figure was none other than Lord Krishna, the divine incarnation of Vishnu, whose Machiavellian moves played a pivotal role in shaping the course of history.

As the war between the Pandavas and the Kauravas loomed on the horizon, Krishna understood that victory could not be achieved through righteousness alone. It would require the mastery of politics, manipulation, and calculated deception. With this understanding, Krishna set forth on a path of Machiavellian maneuvers that would forever alter the destiny of nations.

One of Krishna's most infamous moves was his manipulation of the game of dice that led to the exile of the Pandavas. Sensing the treachery of the Kauravas, Krishna advised Yudhishthira, the eldest Pandava, to participate in the game, knowing full well the consequences of his actions. By luring Yudhishthira into the trap set by the Kauravas, Krishna set the stage for the Pandavas' eventual triumph.

But Krishna's Machiavellian moves did not end there. Throughout the course of the war, he employed a myriad of strategies to weaken the forces of the Kauravas and secure victory for the Pandavas. One such strategy was his orchestration of the death of Abhimanyu, the valiant son of Arjuna, during the battle of Kurukshetra. Recognizing Abhimanyu's prowess as a warrior, Krishna devised a plan to lure him into the Chakravyuha formation, knowing that he would be unable to escape. Though the loss of Abhimanyu was a tragic blow to the Pandavas, it served to demoralize the Kauravas and turn the tide of battle in their favor.

Another Machiavellian move employed by Krishna was his manipulation of alliances and treaties to sow discord among the ranks of the Kauravas. By exploiting the ambitions and rivalries that festered within the enemy camp, Krishna was able to weaken their resolve and fracture their unity. Through his skillful diplomacy and subtle persuasion, he turned former allies against each other, hastening the downfall of the Kauravas.

Yet, amidst the chaos and deception of war, Krishna remained steadfast in his commitment to righteousness. Though his actions may have been Machiavellian in nature, they were ultimately guided by his unwavering devotion to dharma and the preservation of truth and justice.

And so, as the dust settled on the battlefield of Kurukshetra and the echoes of war faded into history, Krishna stood triumphant, his Machiavellian maneuvers paving the way for the restoration of dharma and the triumph of righteousness. For in the grand tapestry of the Mahabharata, it was Krishna's cunning and strategic genius that ensured victory for the forces of good and the defeat of adharma.

☞Key Lessons

1. **The Use of Strategy:** Krishna's actions demonstrate the importance of strategy and planning in achieving one's goals. By carefully orchestrating events and manipulating circumstances, Krishna was able to outmaneuver his adversaries and secure victory for the Pandavas.

2. **Understanding Human Nature:** Krishna's success also highlights the importance of understanding human nature and using that knowledge to influence others. By appealing to the ambitions, fears, and desires of those around him, Krishna was able to manipulate them to his advantage.

3. **The Ends Justify the Means:** Krishna's actions, while seemingly deceptive and manipulative, were ultimately

aimed at achieving a greater good – the restoration of righteousness and the defeat of adharma. This reflects the Machiavellian principle that the ends justify the means.

4. **Adaptability:** Throughout the Mahabharata, Krishna demonstrates a remarkable ability to adapt to changing circumstances and adjust his strategies accordingly. This flexibility is a key component of successful leadership and decision-making.

5. **The Complexity of Morality:** Krishna's actions raise complex moral questions about the nature of right and wrong. While his maneuvers may have been morally questionable, they ultimately led to a positive outcome. This challenges us to think critically about the complexities of morality and ethics.

11.(C)

Managing Internal Conflicts

Lessons from Draupadi's Dispute Resolution

In the illustrious court of Hastinapura, where the destinies of kings and kingdoms were decided, there arose a dispute that would test the bounds of justice and honor. At the heart of this dispute stood Draupadi, the noble and courageous wife of the Pandavas, whose wisdom and strength would ultimately prevail.

The conflict began with the game of dice, where Yudhishthira, the eldest Pandava, wagered and lost everything, including himself and his brothers, to the deceitful Duryodhana, the eldest of the Kauravas. As a result of this treacherous game, Draupadi found herself at the mercy of the Kauravas, who sought to humiliate her in front of the entire court.

In a brazen display of arrogance, Duryodhana commanded Draupadi to sit on his lap, an act that would bring shame upon her and her husbands. But Draupadi, undaunted by the vile intentions of her enemies, refused to comply, calling upon her righteous indignation and unwavering resolve.

Amidst the chaos and confusion that ensued, Draupadi turned to her husbands for aid, seeking justice and protection in their hour of need. But the Pandavas, bound by their honor and duty, were powerless to intervene, having lost themselves in the game of dice.

Faced with the prospect of dishonor and disgrace, Draupadi knew that she must take matters into her own hands. With steely determination and unyielding courage, she turned to the elders of the court, seeking their counsel and guidance in resolving the dispute.

In a masterful display of diplomacy and persuasion, Draupadi appealed to the sense of justice and righteousness that dwelled within each member of the court. With eloquent words and impassioned pleas, she called upon them to uphold the principles of dharma and protect the honor of a woman who had been wronged.

Moved by Draupadi's plight and swayed by her unwavering conviction, the elders of the court began to question the actions of the Kauravas and the validity of the game of dice. Recognizing the injustice that had been perpetrated, they urged Duryodhana to reconsider his actions and seek a peaceful resolution to the dispute.

But Duryodhana, consumed by his pride and ambition, refused to heed their words, choosing instead to escalate the conflict and further antagonize Draupadi and her husbands. And so, the stage was set for a battle of wills, where righteousness would clash with tyranny and honor with deceit.

In the end, it was Draupadi's wisdom and courage that emerged victorious, as she stood firm in the face of adversity and refused to yield to the forces of darkness. Through her unwavering faith in justice and righteousness, she became a beacon of hope and inspiration for all who witnessed her plight, proving that even in the darkest of times, the light of truth and virtue will always prevail.

☞Key Lessons

3. **Courage in Adversity:** Draupadi exemplifies courage in the face of adversity. Despite being in a vulnerable position, she refuses to succumb to humiliation and stands up for her dignity.

4. **Seeking Justice:** Draupadi's actions highlight the importance of seeking justice in the face of wrongdoing. She does not remain passive but actively seeks redress for the injustice done to her.

5. **Diplomacy and Persuasion:** Draupadi's approach to resolving the dispute demonstrates the power of

diplomacy and persuasion. Instead of resorting to violence, she uses her words to appeal to the sense of justice and righteousness of those around her.

6. **Standing Up for Principles:** Draupadi's refusal to compromise her principles, even in the face of great pressure, teaches us the importance of standing up for what is right, no matter the consequences.

7. **The Power of Unity:** Draupadi's story also underscores the power of unity. Despite their initial hesitation, the Pandavas ultimately stand by Draupadi, demonstrating the strength that comes from standing together in the face of adversity.

12. Crisis Management in Times of Turmoil

In the epic tale of the Mahabharata, crisis looms large, testing the resolve and mettle of its characters in times of turmoil. The narrative is replete with instances where leadership, unity, and resilience play pivotal roles in managing crises effectively.

Yudhishthira, the eldest of the Pandavas, exemplifies leadership under pressure. His composure and unwavering adherence to dharma, even in the face of immense personal and familial challenges, serve as a guiding light in times of crisis.

The bond between the Pandavas shines brightest during their exile, a period of immense adversity. Despite being stripped of their kingdom and forced into exile, their unity remains unbroken, showcasing the strength of their bond and their ability to weather the storm together.

Karna's tragic fate, born out of betrayal and injustice, serves as a poignant reminder of the challenges faced in overcoming betrayal. His story highlights the importance of maintaining one's principles and integrity even in the face of betrayal and adversity.

Through these narratives, we glean insights into the art of crisis management in times of turmoil. Leadership, unity, and resilience emerge as key pillars in navigating crises effectively, offering valuable lessons for leaders and individuals alike facing challenges in their own lives.

12.(A)

Leadership Under Pressure

Yudhishthira's Composure

In the ancient land of Bharat, where the echoes of war and the whispers of destiny intertwined, there lived a noble prince whose unwavering composure stood as a beacon of virtue amidst the chaos of the Mahabharata. This prince was Yudhishthira, the eldest of the Pandavas, whose steadfast resolve and unyielding integrity would be tested time and again throughout the epic tale.

The story of Yudhishthira's composure began in the hallowed halls of Hastinapura, where the game of dice unfolded and the fate of kingdoms hung in the balance. As the treacherous dice rolled and the Pandavas wagered their very existence, Yudhishthira remained calm and composed, guided by his unwavering faith in righteousness and dharma.

Even as the dice fell against him and his brothers were lost one by one, Yudhishthira did not waver in his resolve. With a steady hand and a clear mind, he accepted the outcome of the game, recognizing that his fate was but a small part of the larger tapestry of destiny.

But it was not only in times of adversity that Yudhishthira's composure shone brightest. Throughout the trials and tribulations that followed – from the exile in the forest to the battle of Kurukshetra – Yudhishthira remained a pillar of strength and resilience, leading his brothers with wisdom and grace.

In the midst of battle, as the clash of swords and the roar of chariots filled the air, Yudhishthira stood firm, his composure unwavering amidst the chaos of war. With a calm demeanor and a steady gaze, he guided his brothers through the tumultuous tide of battle, inspiring them with his courage and fortitude.

But perhaps the true test of Yudhishthira's composure came in the aftermath of victory, when the Pandavas reclaimed their rightful kingdom and ascended to the throne of Hastinapura. Though the path to victory had been paved with sacrifice and sorrow, Yudhishthira remained steadfast in his commitment to justice and righteousness, ruling with wisdom and compassion as a true Dharmic king.

And so, amidst the trials and tribulations of the Mahabharata, Yudhishthira's composure served as a beacon of hope and inspiration for all who witnessed his journey. Through his unwavering faith in righteousness and his steadfast commitment to dharma, he emerged victorious, proving that true strength lies not in the sword, but in the heart of a noble prince who remains composed in the face of adversity.

☞Key Lessons

1. **Steadfastness in Adversity:** Yudhishthira's composure in the face of adversity teaches us the importance of remaining steadfast and calm, even in the most challenging circumstances.

2. **Faith in Righteousness:** Yudhishthira's unwavering faith in righteousness and dharma reminds us of the importance of upholding moral principles, even when faced with temptation or difficulty.

3. **Leadership by Example:** Yudhishthira's leadership style, characterized by his composure and integrity, serves as an example of how leaders can inspire and guide others through their actions and behavior.

4. **Resilience and Fortitude:** Yudhishthira's resilience and fortitude in the face of adversity demonstrate the importance of perseverance and determination in overcoming challenges.

5. **Wisdom in Decision-Making:** Yudhishthira's wise and thoughtful approach to decision-making, even in the heat of battle, highlights the importance of considering the consequences of our actions and making choices that align with our values.

12.(B)

Unity in Adversity

Pandavas' Bond in Exile

In the ancient land of Bharat, where the winds of destiny whispered tales of honor and betrayal, there existed a bond forged in the crucible of adversity – the bond of brotherhood between the Pandavas. As they embarked on their exile, stripped of their kingdom and riches by the deceitful game of dice, the Pandavas found solace and strength in the unbreakable ties that bound them together.

Their journey through exile began amidst the dense forests that stretched across the kingdom of Hastinapura. With determination etched upon their faces and resolve burning in their hearts, Yudhishthira, Bhima, Arjuna, Nakula, and Sahadeva set forth into the unknown, guided by the timeless principles of righteousness and dharma.

As they ventured deeper into the wilderness, the trials and tribulations of exile tested the limits of their endurance and resilience. Yet, through every hardship and challenge, the Pandavas stood united, their bond unyielding in the face of adversity.

In the depths of the forest, where the canopy of trees obscured the light of day and the cries of wild beasts echoed through the night, the Pandavas found strength in each other's company. With Bhima's unmatched strength, Arjuna's unparalleled skill with the bow, and Yudhishthira's unwavering wisdom, they overcame every obstacle that lay in their path.

But it was not only the physical challenges of exile that tested the Pandavas' bond. As they grappled with the loss of their kingdom and the weight of their exile, they faced internal struggles and doubts that threatened to tear them apart. Yet, through the power of their shared experiences and the bonds of brotherhood that bound them together, they found the strength to persevere.

In the darkest hours of their exile, when despair threatened to engulf their souls and the shadows of doubt loomed large, it was the light of their bond that guided them through the darkness. With each passing day, their resolve grew stronger, their spirits lifted by the knowledge that they were not alone in their struggles.

And so, as they journeyed through the wilderness, the Pandavas forged a bond that transcended the boundaries of time and space, a bond that would carry them through the trials and tribulations that lay ahead. For in the crucible of exile, amidst the shadows of uncertainty and despair, they discovered the true strength of brotherhood – an unbreakable bond that would endure for all eternity.

☞Key Lessons

3. **Strength in Unity:** The Pandavas' bond of brotherhood demonstrates the power of unity in overcoming adversity. Despite facing numerous challenges, their strength and resilience grew stronger when they stood united.

4. **Resilience in the Face of Adversity:** The Pandavas' ability to persevere through the trials of exile teaches us the importance of resilience and determination in overcoming life's challenges.

5. **Support and Dependence:** The Pandavas leaned on each other for support during their exile, highlighting the value of mutual dependence and the strength that comes from having a supportive network.

6. **Adherence to Dharma:** Despite their hardships, the Pandavas remained committed to upholding righteousness and dharma, showing the importance of staying true to one's principles even in difficult times.

7. **The Value of Brotherhood:** Above all, the story emphasizes the deep and enduring bond of brotherhood

that sustained the Pandavas through their exile. It teaches us the value of family and the strength that comes from standing together in the face of adversity.

12.(C)

Overcoming Betrayal

Lessons from Karna's Tragic Fate

In the vast tapestry of the Mahabharata, there existed a character whose tragic fate would leave an indelible mark upon the of history. This character was Karna, the noble-hearted warrior born to a destiny of greatness and sorrow.

Karna's story began amidst the sands of time, where fate conspired to place him on a path fraught with trials and tribulations. Born to Kunti, the mother of the Pandavas, and Surya, the sun god, Karna was abandoned at birth and raised by a charioteer, unaware of his true lineage.

Despite his humble origins, Karna possessed a noble spirit and unmatched skill in the art of warfare. His valor and prowess on the battlefield earned him the admiration of kings and warriors alike, yet his true identity remained shrouded in mystery.

But it was not until the fateful day of the tournament at Hastinapura that Karna's true destiny began to unfold. Disguised as a charioteer's son, Karna arrived at the tournament to showcase his martial prowess and compete for honor and glory. Little did he know that his presence would set into motion a chain of events that would shape the fate of nations.

As the tournament unfolded and the competition grew fierce, Karna emerged as a formidable contender, his skill with the bow rivaling even that of Arjuna, the greatest warrior of his time. Yet, despite his valiant efforts, Karna was denied the recognition and respect that he rightfully deserved, for his lowly birth cast a shadow upon his achievements.

But it was not only the scorn of society that weighed heavily upon Karna's heart. Deep within the recesses of his soul, Karna harbored a sense of betrayal and longing, for he knew not the love of his mother nor the embrace of his true family. And so, he vowed to carve out a place for himself in the world, to prove his worth and earn the respect of those who had spurned him.

Yet, despite his best efforts, Karna's fate remained inexorably tied to the forces of destiny. For when the time came for him to choose sides in the great war of Kurukshetra, Karna found himself torn between loyalty to his friend and benefactor, Duryodhana, and the bonds of blood that tied him to the Pandavas.

In the end, it was Karna's sense of honor and duty that led him to pledge his allegiance to Duryodhana, despite the whispers of doubt that lingered in his heart. And so, he marched into battle alongside his friend and king, prepared to lay down his life in defense of his principles.

But even in the midst of battle, as the clash of swords and the cries of the dying filled the air, Karna's tragic destiny would finally come to pass. For it was on the battlefield of Kurukshetra that Karna would face his greatest adversary – Arjuna, his long-lost brother and the greatest warrior of his time.

In a battle that would echo through the ages, Karna and Arjuna clashed, their swords ringing out like thunder amidst the chaos of war. But despite his valor and skill, Karna could not escape the web of fate that had ensnared him, for he was bound by a vow that would seal his tragic fate.

As the battle raged on, Karna found himself at a crossroads, torn between his duty to his friend and his loyalty to his family. Yet, in the end, it was his sense of honor that would guide him, for he knew that to forsake his principles would be to forsake himself.

And so, with a heavy heart and a steadfast resolve, Karna faced his final destiny, his tragic fate sealed by the choices he had made and the burdens he had borne. For in the end, it was not the battles he won or the victories he achieved that defined him, but the nobility of his spirit and the sacrifices he made in the name of honor and duty.

☞Key Lessons

8. **The Importance of Identity and Self-Worth:** Karna's struggle with his identity and worth teaches us the importance of recognizing our own value, irrespective of societal judgments or circumstances of birth.

9. **The Power of Compassion and Empathy:** Despite facing rejection and betrayal, Karna remained compassionate and empathetic towards others. His story reminds us of the transformative power of compassion and empathy in overcoming personal hardships.

10. **The Complexity of Loyalty and Duty:** Karna's loyalty to Duryodhana, despite knowing the righteousness of the Pandavas' cause, raises questions about the complexities of loyalty and duty. It prompts us to consider the moral implications of our allegiances and actions.

11. **The Tragedy of Pride and Ego:** Karna's downfall can also be attributed to his pride and ego, which blinded him to the truth and led him to make choices that ultimately sealed his tragic fate. His story serves as a cautionary tale about the dangers of unchecked pride and ego.

12. **The Value of Integrity and Honor:** Throughout his life, Karna upheld his principles of integrity and honor, even at great personal cost. His story underscores the importance

of staying true to one's values, even in the face of adversity.

13. **The Role of Fate and Destiny:** Karna's life was shaped by forces beyond his control, highlighting the role of fate and destiny in our lives. His story encourages us to reflect on the balance between fate and free will and how we navigate these forces in our own lives.

13. Intelligence Gathering and Utilization for Strategic Advantage

In the ancient epic of the Mahabharata, the strategic use of intelligence and information plays a crucial role in shaping the course of events. Characters such as Krishna, the Pandavas, and Vidura demonstrate the importance of intelligence gathering and utilization for gaining a strategic advantage.

Krishna, with his divine insight and strategic acumen, adeptly uses information to manipulate events and influence outcomes in the great war of Kurukshetra. His use of spycraft and espionage highlights the strategic advantage that can be gained through the effective use of intelligence.

The Pandavas' scout network, led by Bhima and Satyaki, showcases the importance of tactical reconnaissance in warfare. Their ability to gather valuable information about enemy movements and intentions proves instrumental in shaping their strategies and gaining an edge over their adversaries.

Vidura, known for his wisdom and sage advice, demonstrates the importance of intelligence in decision-making. His counsel to the Kuru dynasty, based on his keen insights and understanding of the political landscape, serves as a testament to the strategic value of intelligence gathering and utilization.

Through these examples, we learn valuable lessons about the strategic advantage that can be gained through the effective use of intelligence. Whether through spycraft, reconnaissance, or wise counsel, the characters of the Mahabharata show us that intelligence gathering and utilization are key components of strategic success in times of conflict and uncertainty.

13.(A)

Spycraft and Espionage

Krishna's Use of Information

In the grand tapestry of the Mahabharata, amidst the clash of empires and the echoes of destiny, there existed a figure whose mastery of information would shape the course of history. This figure was none other than Lord Krishna, the divine incarnation of Vishnu, whose strategic wisdom and foresight were unparalleled in the record of time.

Krishna understood that in the game of war, information was a weapon as powerful as any sword or bow. With his keen intellect and divine insight, he utilized information as a tool to manipulate events and influence the outcome of the conflict between the Pandavas and the Kauravas.

One of Krishna's most famous displays of strategic wisdom came during the peace negotiations before the war of Kurukshetra. As the envoy of the Pandavas, Krishna approached the Kaurava court with a proposal for a peaceful resolution to the conflict. But hidden beneath his words of peace lay a carefully crafted plan to gather valuable information about the enemy's intentions and strengths.

Through his conversations with the Kaurava princes and his observations of their reactions, Krishna gleaned valuable insights into their mindset and strategies. He learned of their weaknesses and vulnerabilities, their fears and insecurities, and used this knowledge to devise a plan that would tilt the scales of war in favor of the Pandavas.

But Krishna's strategic use of information did not end there. Throughout the course of the war, he employed a myriad of tactics to gather intelligence and gain the upper hand over his adversaries. Whether it was through spies and informants planted within the enemy camp or through his divine omniscience, Krishna remained one step ahead of his opponents at every turn.

One such example of Krishna's strategic brilliance came during the battle of Kurukshetra, when he advised Arjuna to target the vulnerable spot on Bhishma's body, knowing that it was the only way to defeat the invincible warrior. With this crucial piece of information, Arjuna was able to turn the tide of battle and secure victory for the Pandavas.

But perhaps the most famous display of Krishna's strategic wisdom came during the climactic moment of the war, when he revealed his divine form to Arjuna on the battlefield of Kurukshetra. In doing so, Krishna not only inspired Arjuna to fight with renewed vigor and determination but also sent a powerful message to the enemy forces – that victory was assured for those who stood on the side of righteousness.

And so, through his strategic use of information and his divine guidance, Krishna ensured that justice prevailed and dharma triumphed over adharma. For in the grand tapestry of the Mahabharata, it was Krishna's wisdom and foresight that illuminated the path to victory and ensured the triumph of righteousness for generations to come.

☞Key Lessons

1. **Information is Power:** Krishna's use of information as a strategic tool demonstrates the power of knowledge in shaping events and influencing outcomes. It highlights the importance of gathering intelligence and using it wisely in decision-making processes.

2. **Strategic Thinking:** Krishna's ability to think strategically and anticipate the actions of his adversaries is a valuable lesson in planning and preparedness. It emphasizes the importance of considering multiple scenarios and being prepared to adapt to changing circumstances.

3. **Effective Communication:** Krishna's skillful communication and diplomacy during peace negotiations showcase the importance of effective communication in resolving conflicts and building alliances. It underscores the value of clear, concise, and persuasive communication in achieving strategic objectives.

4. **Leadership and Vision:** Krishna's leadership and vision in guiding the Pandavas through the challenges of war demonstrate the qualities of a visionary leader. His ability to inspire others, make tough decisions, and stay focused on long-term goals serves as a model for effective leadership.

5. **Divine Intervention:** While Krishna's divine nature played a significant role in his strategic victories, his actions also highlight the importance of faith and spirituality in overcoming adversity. It suggests that a strong sense of purpose and belief can provide the strength and clarity needed to navigate challenging situations.

13.(B)

Tactical Reconnaissance

Pandavas' Scout Network

In the heart of the ancient land of Bharat, where the winds of destiny whispered secrets and the clash of empires echoed through the ages, there existed a network of spies and scouts whose watchful eyes and keen ears served as the silent guardians of the Pandavas. This network, born out of necessity and forged in the fires of war, played a crucial role in shaping the course of the Mahabharata.

At the helm of this covert operation stood Bhima, the mighty warrior of the Pandavas, whose strength and ferocity were matched only by his cunning and resourcefulness. Recognizing the need for timely and accurate intelligence in the midst of war,

Bhima assembled a team of skilled spies and scouts drawn from all corners of the kingdom.

Led by Bhima's trusted lieutenant, the cunning and quick-witted Satyaki, the scout network operated with precision and stealth, gathering information from enemy territories and reporting back to the Pandavas with valuable insights into the movements and intentions of their adversaries.

From the bustling streets of Hastinapura to the remote corners of the wilderness, the scouts of the Pandavas moved unseen and unheard, their identities shrouded in secrecy and their allegiance sworn to the cause of righteousness. Disguised as merchants, travelers, and common laborers, they ventured into enemy territory, gathering information through stealth and subterfuge.

But it was not only the enemy's movements that the scouts monitored. They also kept a watchful eye on the morale and disposition of the Pandavas' own forces, reporting back to Bhima with updates on their readiness and resolve. Through their efforts, Bhima was able to anticipate and address any challenges or obstacles that arose, ensuring that the Pandavas always remained one step ahead of their adversaries.

One of the most crucial moments in the scout network's history came during the build-up to the great war of Kurukshetra. As tensions mounted and battle lines were drawn, Bhima dispatched his scouts to gather intelligence on the enemy's preparations and strengths. Through their efforts, Bhima was able to formulate a strategic plan that would give the Pandavas the upper hand in battle.

But perhaps the most remarkable aspect of the scout network was its unwavering loyalty and commitment to the Pandavas' cause. Despite the dangers and hardships they faced, the scouts remained steadfast in their dedication, willing to risk life and limb in service to their leaders.

And so, as the great war of Kurukshetra raged on, the scout network stood as a testament to the power of information and the importance of vigilance in the face of adversity. Through their tireless efforts and unwavering devotion, they played a crucial role in securing victory for the Pandavas and ensuring that righteousness triumphed over adharma.

☞Key Lessons

1. **The Importance of Intelligence:** The scout network highlights the critical role that intelligence plays in warfare and decision-making. It demonstrates the value of timely and accurate information in anticipating enemy movements and planning strategic responses.

2. **Effective Leadership:** Bhima's leadership of the scout network showcases the qualities of a strong and effective leader. His ability to assemble a skilled team, delegate tasks, and make informed decisions based on intelligence reflects the importance of leadership in managing complex operations.

3. **Stealth and Subterfuge:** The scouts' use of disguises and covert tactics illustrates the importance of stealth and

subterfuge in gathering intelligence. It underscores the need for creativity and adaptability in espionage and reconnaissance.

4. **Loyalty and Commitment:** The unwavering loyalty and commitment of the scouts to the Pandavas' cause highlight the importance of trust and dedication in building a successful team. It emphasizes the value of individuals who are willing to go above and beyond in service to their leaders.

5. **Strategic Advantage:** The scout network's role in providing strategic advantage to the Pandavas demonstrates the impact that intelligence can have on the outcome of a conflict. It underscores the importance of information superiority in achieving military success.

Wisdom of Counsel

Vidura's Sage Advice

In the ancient kingdom of Hastinapura, where the echoes of destiny reverberated through the halls of power, there lived a man whose wisdom and sage advice would shape the course of history. This man was Vidura, the trusted counselor and advisor to the Kuru dynasty, whose words of wisdom were sought by kings and commoners alike.

Vidura's story began amidst the tumultuous political landscape of Hastinapura, where ambition and intrigue threatened to tear the kingdom apart. As the half-brother of King Dhritarashtra and the son of a servant maid, Vidura occupied a unique position within the royal court, his lowly birth contrasting sharply with his towering intellect and moral integrity.

Despite the challenges he faced, Vidura remained steadfast in his commitment to righteousness and justice, serving as a voice of reason and conscience amidst the chaos and corruption that plagued the kingdom. With his keen insight and unwavering principles, he earned the respect and admiration of all who knew him, including his brothers and nephews.

But it was not only within the walls of Hastinapura that Vidura's wisdom shone brightest. Throughout the Mahabharata, he played a crucial role in guiding the destinies of kings and kingdoms, offering sage counsel and advice that would shape the course of events to come.

One of the most famous instances of Vidura's sage advice came during the game of dice, where Yudhishthira, the eldest of the Pandavas, wagered and lost everything to the deceitful Duryodhana. Sensing the treachery of the Kauravas, Vidura warned Dhritarashtra of the dangers of allowing the game to proceed, urging him to intervene and prevent the impending disaster. But Dhritarashtra, blinded by his love for his son and his own ambitions, ignored Vidura's counsel, paving the way for the exile of the Pandavas and the war that would follow.

Throughout the epic tale of the Mahabharata, Vidura's sage advice served as a guiding light in the darkness, offering wisdom and counsel to those who sought his guidance. Whether it was advising Yudhishthira on matters of statecraft or warning Dhritarashtra of the consequences of his actions, Vidura remained a steadfast beacon of moral clarity in a world consumed by greed and ambition.

And so, as the story of the Mahabharata unfolded, Vidura's wisdom continued to illuminate the path of righteousness, guiding the destinies of kings and kingdoms with his sage advice and unwavering principles. For in the grand tapestry of history, it was Vidura's words of wisdom that echoed through the ages, reminding future generations of the timeless virtues of integrity, honor, and moral clarity.

☞ Key Lessons

1. **Integrity and Moral Clarity:** Vidura's unwavering commitment to righteousness and justice, despite his lowly birth and the challenges he faced, highlights the importance of integrity and moral clarity in guiding one's actions.

2. **Wisdom and Insight:** Vidura's sage advice and counsel demonstrate the value of wisdom and insight in navigating complex political and moral dilemmas. His ability to see beyond the surface and understand the deeper implications of actions serves as a model for wise decision-making.

3. **Courage to Speak Truth to Power:** Vidura's willingness to speak truth to power, even when it was unpopular or went against the ambitions of those in authority, underscores the importance of courage and conviction in upholding one's principles.

4. **Role of Counselors and Advisors:** Vidura's role as a trusted counselor and advisor highlights the importance of having wise and impartial advisors in positions of power. His counsel often served as a voice of reason and conscience, guiding laders towards more virtuous and just decisions.

5. **Impact of Individual Actions:** Vidura's actions and advice had a significant impact on the course of events in the Mahabharata. His warnings and counsel, though sometimes ignored, played a crucial role in shaping the destiny of kings and kingdoms.

Conclusion

The Mahabharata stands as a timeless epic that continues to captivate audiences with its rich narrative and profound wisdom. Through its characters and their actions, the Mahabharata offers valuable lessons in strategic leadership that are as relevant today as they were thousands of years ago.

One of the key takeaways from the epic is the importance of visionary leadership, as exemplified by figures like King Dhritarashtra and Lord Krishna. Dhritarashtra's lack of foresight and inability to see beyond his own ambitions ultimately led to the destruction of his dynasty, highlighting the need for leaders to consider the long-term consequences of their decisions. On the other hand, Krishna's strategic acumen and ability to see the bigger picture allowed him to guide the Pandavas to victory, showcasing the impact that visionary leadership can have in times of crisis.

The Mahabharata also emphasizes the importance of adaptability and flexibility in leadership. Characters like Arjuna and Bhima demonstrate the value of being able to adjust tactics and strategies in response to changing circumstances, showing that rigidity can often lead to failure. Additionally, the epic highlights the importance of resilience and perseverance, as seen in the Pandavas' ability to endure years of exile and hardship before ultimately reclaiming their kingdom.

Overall, the Mahabharata serves as a profound testament to the complexities of leadership and the enduring principles of strategy. By studying the strategic leadership displayed by its characters, modern leaders can gain valuable insights into effective decision-making, crisis management, and the qualities that define truly visionary leaders.

(a). Applications in Modern Business and Leadership

The timeless wisdom and strategic insights from the Mahabharata are not confined to ancient battles and royal intrigues. They offer profound lessons that can be applied to modern business and leadership. By examining the actions and decisions of the epic's key characters, contemporary leaders can gain valuable perspectives on how to navigate the complexities of today's corporate world.

Visionary Leadership

In modern business, visionary leadership is crucial for guiding organizations through turbulent times and towards long-term success. Krishna's ability to foresee outcomes and guide the Pandavas with a strategic vision is akin to a CEO steering a company through market disruptions. Leaders must develop a clear vision, anticipate industry trends, and inspire their teams to achieve shared goals, much like Krishna did with his unwavering commitment to dharma and justice.

Adaptability and Flexibility

The Mahabharata underscores the importance of adaptability, a lesson highly relevant in today's fast-paced business environment. Arjuna's ability to master different weapons and tactics can be likened to a business leader's need to be versatile and open to new strategies. In the corporate world, this translates to embracing innovation, being agile in the face of change, and continuously evolving business models to stay competitive.

Resilience and Perseverance

The resilience shown by the Pandavas during their years of exile mirrors the perseverance required in business. Companies often face setbacks and periods of hardship. The key to overcoming these challenges lies in maintaining a strong sense of purpose, learning from failures, and staying committed to long-term objectives. Business leaders can draw inspiration from the Pandavas' unwavering resolve to reclaim their kingdom despite numerous obstacles.

Strategic Thinking

Strategic thinking, as demonstrated by Krishna and Vidura, is essential for effective business leadership. In today's complex market landscape, leaders must analyze competitive forces, anticipate potential threats, and craft strategies that leverage their organization's strengths. Vidura's counsel and Krishna's tactical maneuvers illustrate the importance of informed decision-making and the ability to think several steps ahead.

Ethical Leadership

The Mahabharata places a strong emphasis on ethics and morality, which are equally important in business. Yudhishthira's adherence to dharma despite personal loss highlights the importance of integrity in leadership. Modern leaders must prioritize ethical behavior, build trust with stakeholders, and ensure their actions align with core values. This fosters a culture of transparency and accountability, essential for long-term success.

Building Strong Teams

The unity and collaboration among the Pandavas showcase the power of effective teamwork. In the business context, leaders must cultivate strong, cohesive teams that leverage diverse skills and perspectives. Encouraging collaboration, fostering a supportive environment, and aligning team efforts with organizational goals are critical for achieving success.

Crisis Management

The Mahabharata provides valuable lessons in crisis management, exemplified by Yudhishthira's composure and Krishna's crisis navigation. Modern leaders can learn the importance of staying calm under pressure, making informed decisions swiftly, and maintaining clear communication during crises. Effective crisis management involves anticipating potential challenges, preparing contingency plans, and leading with confidence and empathy.

Intelligence Gathering and Utilization

Krishna's use of information and the Pandavas' scout network highlight the significance of intelligence gathering in strategy formulation. In business, data-driven decision-making is paramount. Leaders must gather and analyze market data, customer insights, and competitive intelligence to inform their strategies. This ensures they stay ahead of trends and make well-informed decisions that drive growth and innovation.

(b). Recapitulation of Strategic Leadership from the Mahabharata:

1. **Visionary Leadership:** King Dhritarashtra's lack of foresight and Krishna's strategic acumen showcase the impact of visionary leadership on the outcome of events.

2. **Adaptability and Flexibility:** Arjuna and Bhima demonstrate the value of being able to adjust tactics and strategies in response to changing circumstances, highlighting the importance of adaptability in leadership.

3. **Resilience and Perseverance:** The Pandavas' ability to endure years of hardship and maintain their resolve serves as a testament to the importance of resilience and perseverance in leadership.

4. **Strategic Thinking:** Characters like Krishna, Vidura, and Bhishma exhibit strategic thinking in their decision-making, emphasizing the importance of strategic acumen in leadership.

5. **Ethics and Morality:** The Mahabharata also underscores the significance of ethical leadership, with characters like Yudhishthira and Draupadi exemplifying the importance of upholding moral values in leadership.

Notes

www.ingramcontent.com/pod-product-compliance
Lightning Source LLC
Chambersburg PA
CBHW071527040426
42452CB00008B/915